The HOME HUNTERS Playbook

I0431689

> **"WHEN YOU GIVE SOMEONE A BOOK, YOU DON'T GIVE HIM JUST PAPER, INK AND GLUE, YOU GIVE HIM POSSIBILITY OF A WHOLE NEW WORLD."**

Table of Contents

PREPARE — 1
You'll find everything needed to PREPARE for your home hunting journey!

- The Home Hunters Process
- How Much Can You Afford?
- Get To Know Your Lender
- Lender Evaluation Form
- Uniform Lender Application
- Insurances & Warranties
- Inspections & Attorneys
- Document Checklist

SEARCH — 16
Now that you are prepared it's time to SEARCH for your perfect home!

- What's your Home Identity?
- Individual Home Evaluation

MOVE — 28
Use this section to plan an efficient, stress free and easy MOVE into your home!

- Moving Timeline Checklist
- Moving To Do List
- Change of Address Checklist
- Things to Sell, Donate or Give
- Moving Box Inventory
- Needs for your Home Checklist

CLEAN — 35
After you've moved in use this section to keep your home CLEAN and maintained!

- Cleaning Checklist
- Seasonal Maintenance Checklist
- Deep Clean Checklist

ORGANIZE — 39
While living in your new home it's important to ORGANIZE all aspects of your life!

- Monthly Budget Worksheet
- Password Keeper
- Warranty Tracker
- Household Purchase Tracker
- Maintenance Tracker
- In Case of Emergency 9-1-1
- Daily Tracker Worksheet
- Household Notes

© The Home Hunters Playbook
© The Home Hunters Playbook

PREPARE
notes

The Home Hunters Process
Welcome to the beginning of an incredible journey!

Congratulations on your journey of being a homeowner! A home is where love resides, memories are created, friends always belong and happiness never ends. The Home Hunters Playbook is here to help you find a home that brings you everlasting happiness! You'll find resources for buying or renting the perfect home for you and your family.

It pays to come into the home-buying process armed with as much information as possible. So that being said, think ahead and consider future needs such as: finances needed, marriage, family additions, job location, schooling, travel requirements, etc.

Buying a home is the most exciting stressful thing you can do. It is an emotional roller coaster. Here is why:
- Sellers can be unreasonable or unknowledgeable about the process.
- Mortgage lenders may reject you.
- A home inspection may have a long list of defects.
- There may be title issues.
- Waiting for acceptance.

First, you'll want to become familiar with types of contracts you will see along the way when executing a real estate sale:

• **Listing Agreements:** a legal contract between a real estate broker and an owner of real property granting the broker the authority to act as the owner's agent in the sale of the property.

• **Buyer Agency Agreements:** a legal contract that is signed between a home buyer and their real estate agent when purchasing a home. The Buyer Agency Agreement outlines duties and obligations of the agent and also ensures that a buyer's agent receives compensation when a sale occurs.

• **Purchase Agreements:** a legal contract between a buyer and a seller -- sometimes stated in the contract as a "purchaser" and "vendor" -- in which the seller sells a stated number of shares at a stated price. The agreement is proof that the sale and its terms were mutually agreed upon.

• **Land Contracts:** An agreement between a buyer and seller of property in which the buyer makes payments toward full ownership (as with a mortgage), but in a land contract, the title or deed is held by the owner until the full payment is made (AKA an installment purchase contract or an installment sale agreement).

• **Option Agreements:** an agreement between a buyer and seller that gives the purchaser of the option the right to buy or sell a particular asset at a later date at an agreed upon price. Option contracts are often used in securities, commodities, and real estate transactions.

©The Home Hunters Playbook

How much can you afford?
Make sure you have the upfront and monthly costs planned out!

You'll hear different advice on what you can afford to borrow depending on who you ask, but a good rule of thumb is to keep to these limits:

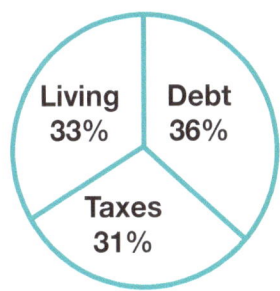

- 36% goes to pay debts. Banks generally advise that your mortgage payment not be more than 28% of your gross monthly income, leaving 8% for other debts like a car loan.

- 31% of your income goes toward taxes. That's the national average.

- 33% goes toward everything else — food, clothes, entertainment, vacations, as well as savings and __ investments that you put away for a rainy day.

Part 1: What can you afford to put down and pay monthly?

Purchase Price of Home	10% Down Payment	Loan Amount	Monthly Payment
$100,000	$10,000	$90,000	$731
$200,000	$20,000	$180,000	$1,462
$300,000	$30,000	$270,000	$2,193
$400,000	$40,000	$360,000	$2,923
$500,000	$50,000	$450,000	$3,656

Desired Purchase Price
$_____

Available Down Payment
$_____

Desired Monthly Payment
$_____

This chart estimates the monthly principal, interest, property taxes and insurance payments assuming a 10% down payment and a 30 year fixed rate mortgage at 5%.

Part 2: One-time fees

Mortgage Down Payment $_____
Typically 5%-20% of home cost.

Rental & Security Deposit $_____
Typically first and last month rent.

Home Appraisal $_____
A professional analysis of the home/property market value ($200-$500).

Home Inspection $_____
A detailed report on the condition of the house, highlighting any significant problems ($200-$1,000).

Termite Inspection $_____
An evaluation of any pest damage ($100).

Origination fees $_____
Fees assessed by the bank to cover the processing of the loan and admin costs (0.5% - 2% of loan).

Closing fees $_____
Bank fees and third-party vendor fees that may include: attorneys, settlement, title insurance, recording, appraisal, etc (2% - 6% of loan).

Moving costs $_____
Varies depending on how far you're going, how much to move and if you hire a company to assist you.

Utility Deposits $_____
Could be required due to poor credit or first time buyer/renter for electric, water, cable, etc.

Total One Time fees $_____

Part 3: Monthly Cash Needed

Monthly Payment $_____
Mortgage principal, interest & taxes or rent.

Mortgage Insurance $_____
Most lenders will require if down payment is less than 20%.

Maintenance $_____
Typically covers the cost ($200-$350/mo) of insurance, taxes, maintenance (lawn care and exterior care).

HOA dues $_____
Typically covers fees associated with maintaining the neighborhood and clubhouse.

Utilities $_____
Water, gas, electric, garbage, recycling, cable, phone, etc.

Other Debts $_____
Such as auto, student loans, credit cards.

Other Insurances $_____
Such as life, health, auto, renters, etc.

Other Expenses $_____
Groceries, entertainment, education, etc.

Property Maintenance $_____
If not covered by an association these can range from $100-$500/mo, depending on size.

Home Maintenance $_____
depending on the age of your home there could be periodic repairs and maintenance needed, budget $100-$500/mo.

Monthly Cash Needed $_____

©The Home Hunters Playbook

Get to know your Lender
Which one is right for you?

What is a Lender? A Mortgage Lender is the term used to describe companies, institutions and organizations who loan money to people for the purchase of real estate. These include banks, credit unions, trust companies, life insurance companies or a private company that lends money to buy land, houses and other real estate.

Which Mortgage Is Best For You?

CONVENTIONAL
- Good to Excellent Credit
- Fixed or Adjustable Rates
- Typical term is 15-30 years
- Minimum down payment required
- 97% Financing available for primary residence, 2nd home, investment property, non-owner occupied

VETERAN AFFAIRS (VA)
- Available to veterans, reservists, active duty personnel and surviving spouses of veterans
- No down payment required
- 100% financing available
- Reduced interest rates
- 30 & 15 year fixed rate loans
- No mortgage insurance premiums

FHA
- 3.5% down payment
- Low minimum credit score
- Fixed or adjustable rates
- Lower closing costs & payment
- No prepayment penalty
- Streamlined for refinances

JUMBO
- Available for loans up to $5 million
- Fixed & adjustable rates
- Primary or vacation homes

USDA
- Available to rural property owners by the Department of Agriculture
- No down payment required
- Simple qualification

203K
- FHA qualified property
- Funds for home improvement can be included in the loan
- Owner occupied only properties
- FHA down payment of 3.5%
- HUD Repos are eligible

The first step in the home buying process is to select who will offer more than just a competitive rate and fee pricing, but also keep your best interest in hand.

Ask your agent for referrals. Lenders are not allowed to compensate agents for referrals. So this means there's no conflict of interest and your agent would refer you to the top lenders who perform the best because you deserve the best.

Get pre-approved for a mortgage. Time to prospect mortgage lenders. Mortgage lenders will have questions for you, so be prepared:

Identify a Buyer's Agent
Whatever you do don't try this on your own!

A Buyer's Agent has resources, contacts, and tools that would be able to help make the search quicker. A buyer's agent most of the time is paid by the seller, and they have your best interest at hand.

Do not call a listing agent in hopes they have your interest at hand. They are looking for a buyer and you just gave them the opportunity to earn two commissions, and they cannot disclose anything that could take away from their seller's interest.

Ask friends and family for recommendations, or search for agents in the area you are looking to purchase. Always read reviews. Ask questions – just because an agent possesses a license is no guarantee your agent is competent.

The buyer's agent you choose will represent only you and have a fiduciary responsibility to look out for your best interest. Once you tell them they're your preferred agent they will present you with a Buyer's Broker Agreement. Remember it is the seller who pays the agent.

Potential Buyer Agents:

Name: _____ Email: _____
Mobile Phone: _____ Office Phone: _____
Website: _____ Facebook: _____
Notes: _____

Name: _____ Email: _____
Mobile Phone: _____ Office Phone: _____
Website: _____ Facebook: _____
Notes: _____

Name: _____ Email: _____
Mobile Phone: _____ Office Phone: _____
Website: _____ Facebook: _____
Notes: _____

Lender Evaluation Form

Use one page per lender and find the best one for your long term needs!

Company:

Representative:

Address:

City, State, Zip:

Phone:

Email:

Is the company or lender local? Within driving distance?

Who do you know that has used this lender representative (person, not the company) and what was their experience like?

We say this because everyone has worked with Wells Fargo but not everyone has worked with Dena Humphries. It's the lender that makes or breaks a loan, not the company most of the time.

Is this lender referred from your agent?

Agents are your best bet in getting a quality lender since they work with them constantly, and know the good from the bad. Lenders are not allowed to compensate agents for referrals. So this means there's no conflict of interest and your agent would refer you to the top lenders who perform the best because you deserve the best.

What programs does the lender offer?

Loan Programs are loan options that feature flexible qualifying criteria and enable borrowers to make low down payments or helps them in the buying process.

What is the normal time frame to close a loan?

Normal process for USDA loans is 45-60 days. Some loan programs are 30-45 days. FHA and Conventional loans are on average 30 days unless they have problems with the loan like, appraisal and/or title issues or if the customer is not quickly getting the documents that are asked for.

©The Home Hunters Playbook

Lender Evaluation Form
Use one page per lender and find the best one for your long term needs!

Company:
Address:
Phone:
Representative:
City, State, Zip:
Email:

Is the company or lender local? Within driving distance?

Who do you know that has used this lender representative (person, not the company) and what was their experience like?
We say this because everyone has worked with Wells Fargo but not everyone has worked with Dena Humphries. It's the lender that makes or breaks a loan, not the company most of the time.

Is this lender referred from your agent?
Agents are your best bet in getting a quality lender since they work with them constantly, and know the good from the bad. Lenders are not allowed to compensate agents for referrals. So this means there's no conflict of interest and your agent would refer you to the top lenders who perform the best because you deserve the best.

What programs does the lender offer?
Loan Programs are loan options that feature flexible qualifying criteria and enable borrowers to make low down payments or helps them in the buying process.

What is the normal time frame to close a loan?
Normal process for USDA loans is 45-60 days. Some loan programs are 30-45 days. FHA and Conventional loans are on average 30 days unless they have problems with the loan like, appraisal and/or title issues or if the customer is not quickly getting the documents that are asked for.

Lender Evaluation Form
Use one page per lender and find the best one for your long term needs!

Company:

Address:

Phone:

Representative:

City, State, Zip:

Email:

Is the company or lender local? Within driving distance?

Who do you know that has used this lender representative (person, not the company) and what was their experience like?
We say this because everyone has worked with Wells Fargo but not everyone has worked with Dena Humphries. It's the lender that makes or breaks a loan, not the company most of the time.

Is this lender referred from your agent?
Agents are your best bet in getting a quality lender since they work with them constantly, and know the good from the bad. Lenders are not allowed to compensate agents for referrals. So this means there's no conflict of interest and your agent would refer you to the top lenders who perform the best because you deserve the best.

What programs does the lender offer?
Loan Programs are loan options that feature flexible qualifying criteria and enable borrowers to make low down payments or helps them in the buying process.

What is the normal time frame to close a loan?
Normal process for USDA loans is 45-60 days. Some loan programs are 30-45 days. FHA and Conventional loans are on average 30 days unless they have problems with the loan like; appraisal and/or title issues or if the customer is not quickly getting the documents that are asked for.

©The Home Hunters Playbook

Uniform Lender Application (1)
Complete this and ask your agent any questions before applying!

This application is designed to be completed by the applicant(s) with the Lender's assistance. Applicants should complete this form as "Borrower" or "Co-Borrower," as applicable. Co-Borrower information must also be provided (and the appropriate box checked) when ☐ the income or assets of a person other than the Borrower (including the Borrower's spouse) will be used as a basis for loan qualification or ☐ the income or assets of the Borrower's spouse or other person who has community property rights pursuant to state law will not be used as a basis for loan qualification, but his or her liabilities must be considered because the spouse or other person has community property rights pursuant to applicable law and Borrower resides in a community property state, the security property is located in a community property state, or the Borrower is relying on other property located in a community property state as a basis for repayment of the loan.

If this is an application for joint credit, Borrower and Co-Borrower each agree that we intend to apply for joint credit (sign below):

_____ _____
Borrower   Co-Borrower

I. TYPE OF MORTGAGE AND TERMS OF LOAN

Mortgage Applied for:	☐ VA ☐ FHA	☐ Conventional ☐ USDA/Rural Housing Service	☐ Other (explain):	Agency Case Number	Lender Case Number
Amount $		Interest Rate %	No. of Months	Amortization Type: ☐ Fixed Rate ☐ GPM	☐ Other (explain) ☐ ARM (type)

II. PROPERTY INFORMATION AND PURPOSE OF LOAN

Subject Property Address (street, city, state & ZIP)				No. of Units
Legal Description of Subject Property (attach description if necessary)				Year Built

Purpose of Loan	☐ Purchase ☐ Refinance	☐ Construction ☐ Construction-Permanent	☐ Other (explain):	Property will be: ☐ Primary Residence ☐ Secondary Residence ☐ Investment

Complete this line if construction or construction-permanent loan.

Year Lot Acquired	Original Cost $	Amount Existing Liens $	(a) Present Value of Lot $	(b) Cost of Improvements $	Total (a + b) $

Complete this line if this is a refinance loan.

Year Acquired	Original Cost $	Amount Existing Liens $	Purpose of Refinance	Describe Improvements Cost: $	☐ made ☐ to be made

Title will be held in what Name(s)	Manner in which Title will be held	Estate will be held in: ☐ Fee Simple ☐ Leasehold (show expiration date)

Source of Down Payment, Settlement Charges, and/or Subordinate Financing (explain)

III. BORROWER INFORMATION

	Borrower				Co-Borrower		
Borrower's Name (include Jr. or Sr. if applicable)				Co-Borrower's Name (include Jr. or Sr. if applicable)			
Social Security Number	Home Phone (incl. area code)	DOB (mm/dd/yyyy)	Yrs. School	Social Security Number	Home Phone (incl. area code)	DOB (mm/dd/yyyy)	Yrs. School
☐ Married ☐ Separated	☐ Unmarried (include single, divorced, widowed)	Dependents (not listed by Co-Borrower) no. ages		☐ Married ☐ Separated	☐ Unmarried (include single, divorced, widowed)	Dependents (not listed by Borrower) no. ages	
Present Address (street, city, state, ZIP) ☐ Own ☐ Rent ___ No. Yrs.				Present Address (street, city, state, ZIP) ☐ Own ☐ Rent ___ No. Yrs.			
Mailing Address, if different from Present Address				Mailing Address, if different from Present Address			

If residing at present address for less than two years, complete the following:

Former Address (street, city, state, ZIP) ☐ Own ☐ Rent ___ No. Yrs.	Former Address (street, city, state, ZIP) ☐ Own ☐ Rent ___ No. Yrs.

IV. EMPLOYMENT INFORMATION

Borrower			Co-Borrower		
Name & Address of Employer	☐ Self Employed	Yrs. on this job Yrs. employed in this line of work/profession	Name & Address of Employer	☐ Self Employed	Yrs. on this job Yrs. employed in this line of work/profession
Position/Title/Type of Business		Business Phone (incl. area code)	Position/Title/Type of Business		Business Phone (incl. area code)

If employed in current position for less than two years or if currently employed in more than one position, complete the following:

©The Home Hunters Playbook

Uniform Lender Application (2)
Complete this and ask your agent any questions before applying!

Borrower			IV. EMPLOYMENT INFORMATION (cont'd)	Co-Borrower	
Name & Address of Employer	☐ Self Employed	Dates (from – to)	Name & Address of Employer	☐ Self Employed	Dates (from – to)
		Monthly Income $			Monthly Income $
Position/Title/Type of Business		Business Phone (incl. area code)	Position/Title/Type of Business		Business Phone (incl. area code)
Name & Address of Employer	☐ Self Employed	Dates (from – to)	Name & Address of Employer	☐ Self Employed	Dates (from – to)
		Monthly Income $			Monthly Income $
Position/Title/Type of Business		Business Phone (incl. area code)	Position/Title/Type of Business		Business Phone (incl. area code)

V. MONTHLY INCOME AND COMBINED HOUSING EXPENSE INFORMATION

Gross Monthly Income	Borrower	Co-Borrower	Total	Combined Monthly Housing Expense	Present	Proposed
Base Empl. Income*	$	$	$	Rent	$	
Overtime				First Mortgage (P&I)		$
Bonuses				Other Financing (P&I)		
Commissions				Hazard Insurance		
Dividends/Interest				Real Estate Taxes		
Net Rental Income				Mortgage Insurance		
Other (before completing, see the notice in "describe other income," below)				Homeowner Assn. Dues		
				Other:		
Total	$	$	$	Total	$	$

* Self Employed Borrower(s) may be required to provide additional documentation such as tax returns and financial statements.

Describe Other Income *Notice:* Alimony, child support, or separate maintenance income need not be revealed if the Borrower (B) or Co-Borrower (C) does not choose to have it considered for repaying this loan.

B/C		Monthly Amount
		$

VI. ASSETS AND LIABILITIES

This Statement and any applicable supporting schedules may be completed jointly by both married and unmarried Co-Borrowers if their assets and liabilities are sufficiently joined so that the Statement can be meaningfully and fairly presented on a combined basis, otherwise, separate Statements and Schedules are required. If the Co-Borrower section was completed about a non-applicant spouse or other person, this Statement and supporting schedules must be completed about that spouse or other person also.

Completed ☐ Jointly ☐ Not Jointly

ASSETS Description	Cash or Market Value	Liabilities and Pledged Assets. List the creditor's name, address, and account number for all outstanding debts, including automobile loans, revolving charge accounts, real estate loans, alimony, child support, stock pledges, etc. Use continuation sheet, if necessary. Indicate by (*) those liabilities, which will be satisfied upon sale of real estate owned or upon refinancing of the subject property.		
Cash deposit toward purchase held by:	$			
List checking and savings accounts below		LIABILITIES	Monthly Payment & Months Left to Pay	Unpaid Balance
Name and address of Bank, S&L, or Credit Union		Name and address of Company	$ Payment/Months	$
Acct. no.	$	Acct. no.		
Name and address of Bank, S&L, or Credit Union		Name and address of Company	$ Payment/Months	$
Acct. no.	$	Acct. no.		
Name and address of Bank, S&L, or Credit Union		Name and address of Company	$ Payment/Months	$
Acct. no.	$	Acct. no.		

©The Home Hunters Playbook

Uniform Lender Application (3)
Complete this and ask your agent any questions before applying!

VI. ASSETS AND LIABILITIES (cont'd)

Assets		Liabilities		
Name and address of Bank, S&L, or Credit Union		Name and address of Company	$ Payment/Months	$
Acct. no.	$	Acct. no.		
Stocks & Bonds (Company name/ number & description)	$	Name and address of Company	$ Payment/Months	$
		Acct. no.		
Life insurance net cash value Face amount: $	$	Name and address of Company	$ Payment/Months	$
Subtotal Liquid Assets	$			
Real estate owned (enter market value from schedule of real estate owned)	$			
Vested interest in retirement fund	$			
Net worth of business(es) owned (attach financial statement)	$	Acct. no.		
Automobiles owned (make and year)	$	Alimony/Child Support/Separate Maintenance Payments Owed to:	$	
Other Assets (itemize)	$	Job-Related Expense (child care, union dues, etc.)	$	
		Total Monthly Payments	$	
Total Assets a.	$	Net Worth (a minus b) ▶ $	**Total Liabilities b.**	$

Schedule of Real Estate Owned (If additional properties are owned, use continuation sheet.)

Property Address (enter S if sold, PS if pending sale or R if rental being held for income) ▼	Type of Property	Present Market Value	Amount of Mortgages & Liens	Gross Rental Income	Mortgage Payments	Insurance, Maintenance, Taxes & Misc.	Net Rental Income
		$	$	$	$	$	$
Totals		$	$	$	$	$	$

List any additional names under which credit has previously been received and indicate appropriate creditor name(s) and account number(s):

Alternate Name	Creditor Name	Account Number

VII. DETAILS OF TRANSACTION

a.	Purchase price	$
b.	Alterations, improvements, repairs	
c.	Land (if acquired separately)	
d.	Refinance (incl. debts to be paid off)	
e.	Estimated prepaid items	
f.	Estimated closing costs	
g.	PMI, MIP, Funding Fee	
h.	Discount (if Borrower will pay)	
i.	Total costs (add items a through h)	

VIII. DECLARATIONS

If you answer "Yes" to any questions a through i, please use continuation sheet for explanation.

	Borrower		Co-Borrower	
	Yes	No	Yes	No
a. Are there any outstanding judgments against you?	☐	☐	☐	☐
b. Have you been declared bankrupt within the past 7 years?	☐	☐	☐	☐
c. Have you had property foreclosed upon or given title or deed in lieu thereof in the last 7 years?	☐	☐	☐	☐
d. Are you a party to a lawsuit?	☐	☐	☐	☐
e. Have you directly or indirectly been obligated on any loan which resulted in foreclosure, transfer of title in lieu of foreclosure, or judgment?	☐	☐	☐	☐

(This would include such loans as home mortgage loans, SBA loans, home improvement loans, educational loans, manufactured (mobile) home loans, any mortgage, financial obligation, bond, or loan guarantee. If "Yes," provide details, including date, name, and address of Lender, FHA or VA case number, if any, and reasons for the action.)

Uniform Lender Application (4)
Complete this and ask your agent any questions before applying!

VII. DETAILS OF TRANSACTION

j.	Subordinate financing	
k.	Borrower's closing costs paid by Seller	
l.	Other Credits (explain)	
m.	Loan amount (exclude PMI, MIP, Funding Fee financed)	
n.	PMI, MIP, Funding Fee financed	
o.	Loan amount (add m & n)	
p.	Cash from/to Borrower (subtract j, k, l & o from i)	

VIII. DECLARATIONS

If you answer "Yes" to any question a through i, please use continuation sheet for explanation.

		Borrower Yes / No	Co-Borrower Yes / No
f.	Are you presently delinquent or in default on any Federal debt or any other loan, mortgage, financial obligation, bond, or loan guarantee?	☐ ☐	☐ ☐
g.	Are you obligated to pay alimony, child support, or separate maintenance?	☐ ☐	☐ ☐
h.	Is any part of the down payment borrowed?	☐ ☐	☐ ☐
i.	Are you a co-maker or endorser on a note?	☐ ☐	☐ ☐
j.	Are you a U.S. citizen?	☐ ☐	☐ ☐
k.	Are you a permanent resident alien?	☐ ☐	☐ ☐
l.	**Do you intend to occupy the property as your primary residence?** If "Yes," complete question m below.	☐ ☐	☐ ☐
m.	Have you had an ownership interest in a property in the last three years? (1) What type of property did you own—principal residence (PR), second home (SH), or investment property (IP)? (2) How did you hold title to the home—by yourself (S), jointly with your spouse (SP), or jointly with another person (O)?	☐ ☐	☐ ☐

IX. ACKNOWLEDGEMENT AND AGREEMENT

Each of the undersigned specifically represents to Lender and to Lender's actual or potential agents, brokers, processors, attorneys, insurers, servicers, successors and assigns and agrees and acknowledges that: (1) the information provided in this application is true and correct as of the date set forth opposite my signature and that any intentional or negligent misrepresentation of this information contained in this application may result in civil liability, including monetary damages, to any person who may suffer any loss due to reliance upon any misrepresentation that I have made on this application, and/or in criminal penalties including, but not limited to, fine or imprisonment or both under the provisions of Title 18, United States Code, Sec. 1001, et seq.; (2) the loan requested pursuant to this application (the "Loan") will be secured by a mortgage or deed of trust on the property described in this application; (3) the property will not be used for any illegal or prohibited purpose or use; (4) all statements made in this application are made for the purpose of obtaining a residential mortgage loan; (5) the property will be occupied as indicated in this application; (6) the Lender, its servicers, successors or assigns may retain the original and/or an electronic record of this application, whether or not the Loan is approved; (7) the Lender and its agents, brokers, insurers, servicers, successors, and assigns may continuously rely on the information contained in the application, and I am obligated to amend and/or supplement the information provided in this application if any of the material facts that I have represented herein should change prior to closing of the Loan; (8) in the event that my payments on the Loan become delinquent, the Lender, its servicers, successors or assigns may, in addition to any other rights and remedies that it may have relating to such delinquency, report my name and account information to one or more consumer reporting agencies; (9) ownership of the Loan and/or administration of the Loan account may be transferred with such notice as may be required by law; (10) neither Lender nor its agents, brokers, insurers, servicers, successors or assigns has made any representation or warranty, express or implied, to me regarding the property or the condition or value of the property; and (11) my transmission of this application as an "electronic record" containing my "electronic signature," as those terms are defined in applicable federal and/or state laws (excluding audio and video recordings), or my facsimile transmission of this application containing a facsimile of my signature, shall be as effective, enforceable and valid as if a paper version of this application were delivered containing my original written signature.

Acknowledgement. Each of the undersigned hereby acknowledges that any owner of the Loan, its servicers, successors and assigns, may verify or reverify any information contained in this application or obtain any information or data relating to the Loan, for any legitimate business purpose through any source, including a source named in this application or a consumer reporting agency.

Borrower's Signature X	Date	Co-Borrower's Signature X	Date

X. INFORMATION FOR GOVERNMENT MONITORING PURPOSES

The following information is requested by the Federal Government for certain types of loans related to a dwelling in order to monitor the lender's compliance with equal credit opportunity, fair housing and home mortgage disclosure laws. You are not required to furnish this information, but are encouraged to do so. The law provides that a lender may not discriminate either on the basis of this information, or on whether you choose to furnish it. If you furnish the information, please provide both ethnicity and race. For race, you may check more than one designation. If you do not furnish ethnicity, race, or sex, under Federal regulations, this lender is required to note the information on the basis of visual observation and surname if you have made this application in person. If you do not wish to furnish the information, please check the box below. (Lender must review the above material to assure that the disclosures satisfy all requirements to which the lender is subject under applicable state law for the particular type of loan applied for.)

BORROWER ☐ I do not wish to furnish this information
- Ethnicity: ☐ Hispanic or Latino ☐ Not Hispanic or Latino
- Race: ☐ American Indian or Alaska Native ☐ Asian ☐ Black or African American ☐ Native Hawaiian or Other Pacific Islander ☐ White
- Sex: ☐ Female ☐ Male

CO-BORROWER ☐ I do not wish to furnish this information
- Ethnicity: ☐ Hispanic or Latino ☐ Not Hispanic or Latino
- Race: ☐ American Indian or Alaska Native ☐ Asian ☐ Black or African American ☐ Native Hawaiian or Other Pacific Islander ☐ White
- Sex: ☐ Female ☐ Male

To be Completed by Loan Originator:
This information was provided:
- ☐ In a face-to-face interview
- ☐ In a telephone interview
- ☐ By the applicant and submitted by fax or mail
- ☐ By the applicant and submitted via e-mail or the Internet

Loan Originator's Signature X		Date
Loan Originator's Name (print or type)	Loan Originator Identifier	Loan Originator's Phone Number (including area code)
Loan Origination Company's Name	Loan Origination Company Identifier	Loan Origination Company's Address

Insurances & Warranties
Understand the difference and be a smart shopper!

Home warranty and home insurance products may come across as the same, but they are totally different. The coverage, cost, terms and conditions vary greatly. Home insurance is forced in some cases whereas home warranty is a recommended choice.

Home insurance policies cover damages caused by fire, theft, tornadoes, and more. It's important to know the difference between the types of policies so that you don't buy too much or not enough coverage for the area in which you will live.

An HO3 policy covers the structure of your home, but not the contents within. There may be exceptions so check each individual policy for the small print!

HO5 coverage includes everything that is included in an HO3 policy, but its applied to the structure and the property within your home, including your furniture, clothes, and appliances. Although an HO5 policy is the most comprehensive available, it does not include coverage for earthquakes or floods. HO5 insurance policies are available to homes that were either built within the last 30 years or renovated within 40 years, and they typically cover any damages at replacement cost. Refer to your policy for the exact definition and explanation of replacement cost. List a few options below of different insurance carriers:

Name: _____ Company: _____
Phone: _____ Website: _____

Name: _____ Company: _____
Phone: _____ Website: _____

Name: _____ Company: _____
Phone: _____ Website: _____

Home warranty offers protection for your major appliances, as well as plumbing and electrical units. It covers the cost of repairing or replacing major household appliances in case they break down, provided they meet the terms and conditions of the home service contract.

Where can you buy insurance?

The majority of insurance companies allow for online interaction whether that company sells direct to the consumer or through an agent. Some people may believe that purchasing insurance directly from a company results in a lower price. The task of shopping for your insurance is one of those duties that can result in a much better rate through an Independent Agent, than the efforts necessary to seek quotes yourself through a company directly.

Inspections & Attorneys
Know the difference and ask for referrals from your agent!

Why have a licensed and insured home inspection?

A home inspection is an inexpensive way to discover the condition of a home. It is important to conduct a home inspection to avoid a costly mistake by purchasing a property in need of major repairs. A good home inspection will assist a buyer in understanding exactly what they are about to purchase.

Home inspections and appraisals play key role, but separate roles in the home buying process. The lender requires the appraiser to observe the home for a value of the home. The home buyer invests in the inspector's evaluation which also consists of testing mechanical systems/major appliances, and giving a certified report. A home inspector doesn't do termite and pest detection but can let you know of damages they find from termites.

An appraisal isn't a substitute for a professional home inspection in fact they have some key differences. The appraiser formulates an opinion of the property's value for the lender, while the inspector educates the buyer about the condition of the home and its major components. The appraiser is primarily focused on the value of the home whereas the inspector keys in on the home's condition with an eye toward both existing and potential future problems. List a few options you'll be getting estimates from:

Name: _____ Company: _____
Phone: _____ Email: _____
Name: _____ Company: _____
Phone: _____ Email: _____
Name: _____ Company: _____
Phone: _____ Email: _____

Notes: _____

What is a Closing Attorney?

Closing attorneys represent the lender to make certain that the lenders documents are correctly executed. Upon receipt of a real estate purchase agreement the closing attorney will begin to check the title to the property being sold. The closing attorney creates lines of communication between all parties involved for the real estate closing. During closing the attorney is there to explain documents in great details and answer questions.

Document Checklist
Gather these for an easy application process!

Below you'll find the documents you'll need for renting or purchasing a home. With renting you'll most likely need less than what you see here but it's always better to be over prepared than trying to find things the last minute. Keep all of these in a single place for easy reference during your home hunting journey!

IDENTITY & INCOME VERIFICATION

- ○ Full legal name, Social Security number, and birth date (in some cases, you may be asked to provide a copy of your Social Security card)
- ○ Phone number, email address, and current and former residential mailing addresses over the last two years
- ○ Primary and secondary income amounts and sources
- ○ Government-issued photo ID
- ○ Name, addresses, and phone numbers of all employers over the last two years
- ○ Values of bank, retirement, investment, and other asset based accounts
- ○ Monthly debt obligations
- ○ Address of property being purchased, year built, estimated down-payment amount, and purchase price
- ○ Estimates of annual property taxes, homeowners insurance, and any homeowner association dues

INCOME/TAX DOCUMENTS

- ○ IRS Form 4506-T — Request for tax transcript, completed, signed and dated
- ○ Pay stubs covering the last 30 days
- ○ W-2s for the past two years
- ○ Federal tax returns (1040s) for the past two years (3 years if self employed)
- ○ Profit and loss statements if self employed
- ○ List of all business assests & debts
- ○ Investment account statements
- ○ Asset/bank statements — Most recent two months' statements for all accounts listed on the application (include all pages of the statement, including ones that are blank)
- ○ Written explanation if employed less than two years or employment gap exists within the last two years
- ○ Child support or alimony payments

CREDIT VERIFICATION

- ○ Credit Report from the past 30 days
- ○ Explanation letters for late payments, collections, judgments, or other derogatory items in credit history
- ○ Payment history for public utilities, phone, cable TV, car insurance, and other expenses
- ○ Source of funds documentation for any large deposits on asset or bank statements

OTHER INFORMATION NEEDED

- ○ Homeowners insurance - agent's name, phone, company and coverage
- ○ Purchase contract signed by all parties
- ○ _____
- ○ _____
- ○ _____

©The Home Hunters Playbook

SEARCH
notes

What's your home identity?

Select which home styles you like the most!

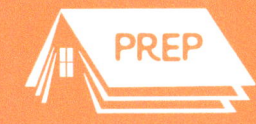

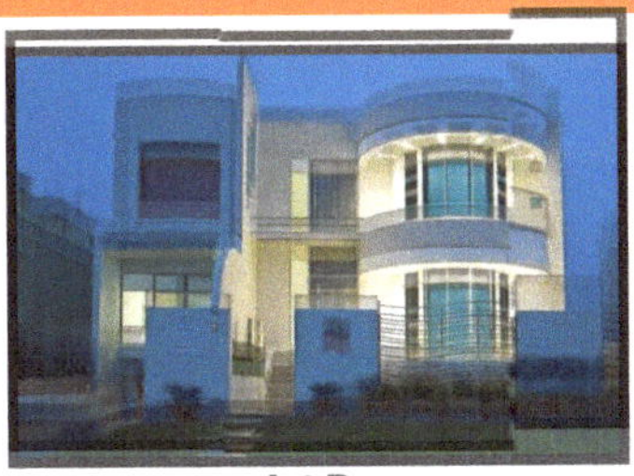
Art Deco

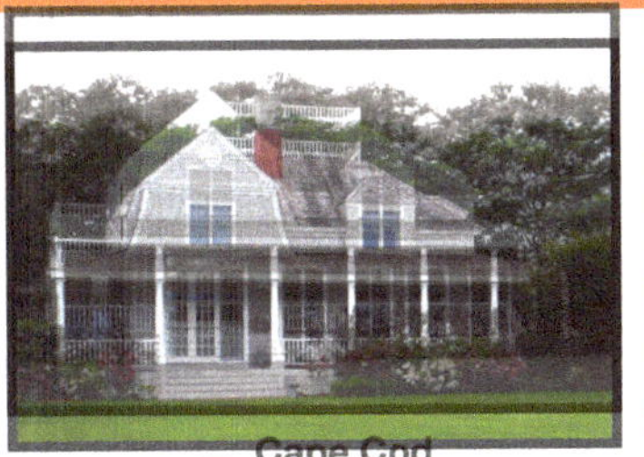
Cape Cod

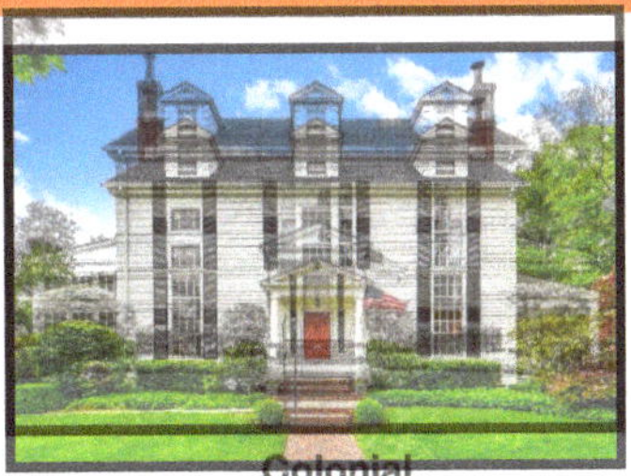
Colonial

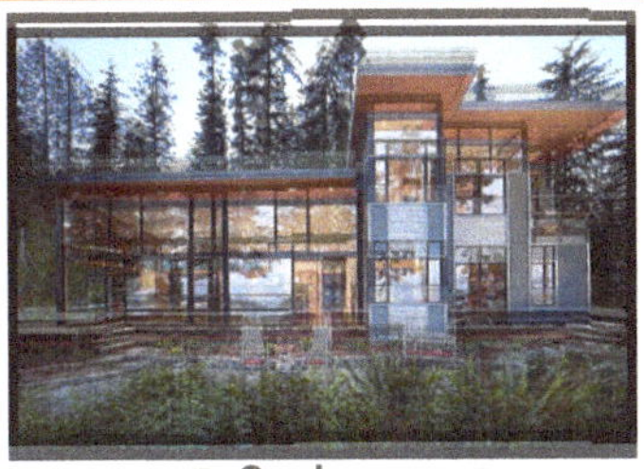
Contemporary

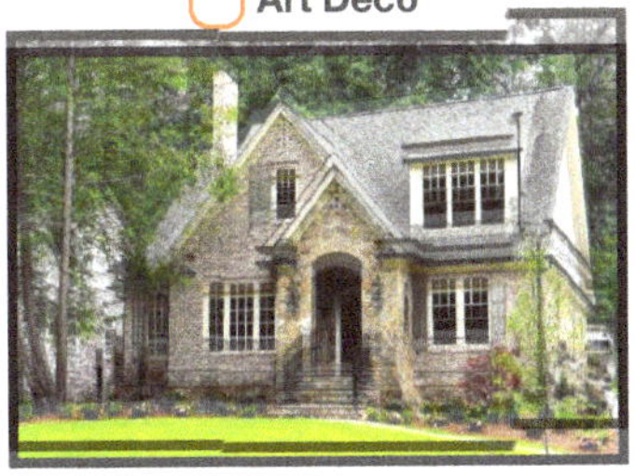
Cottage

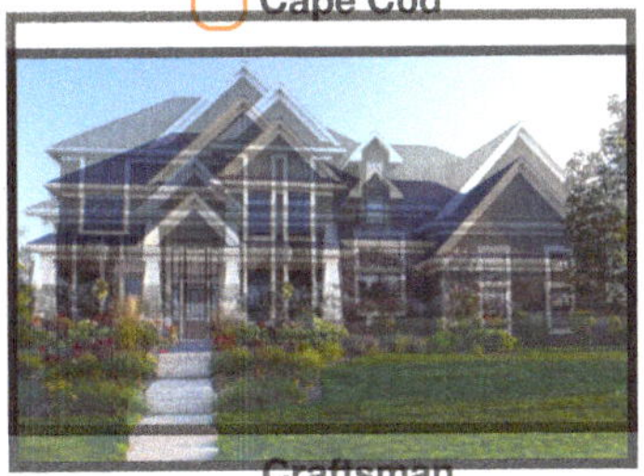
Craftsman

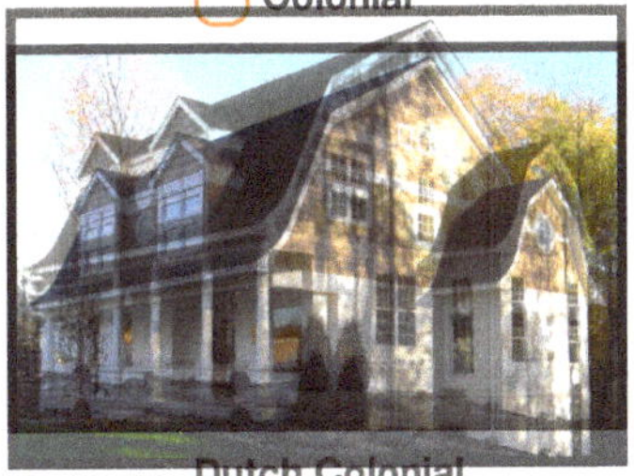
Dutch Colonial

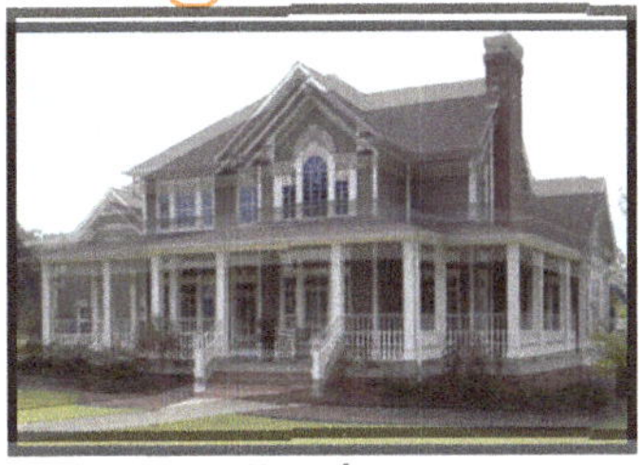
Farmhouse

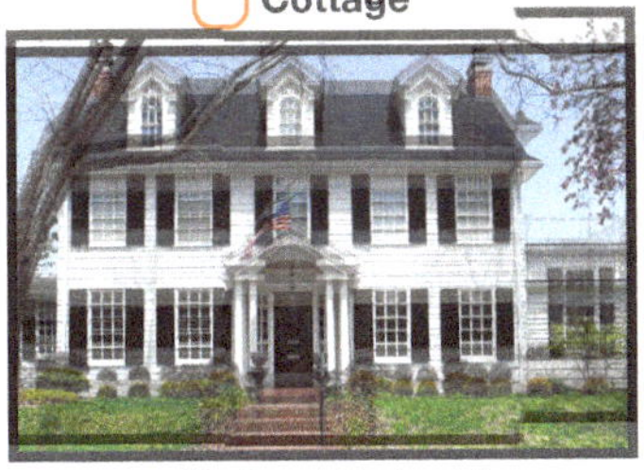
Federal Colonial

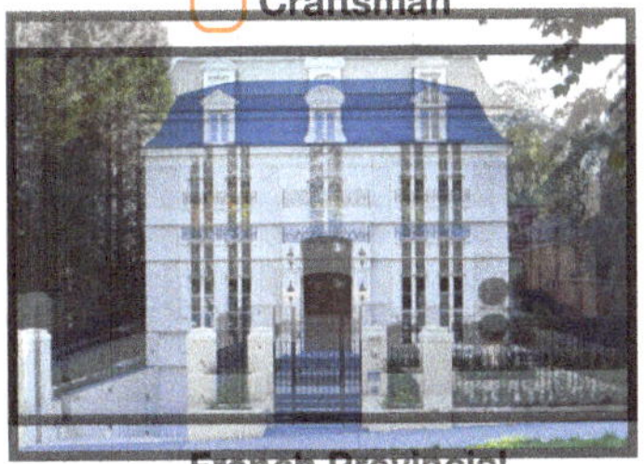
French Provincial

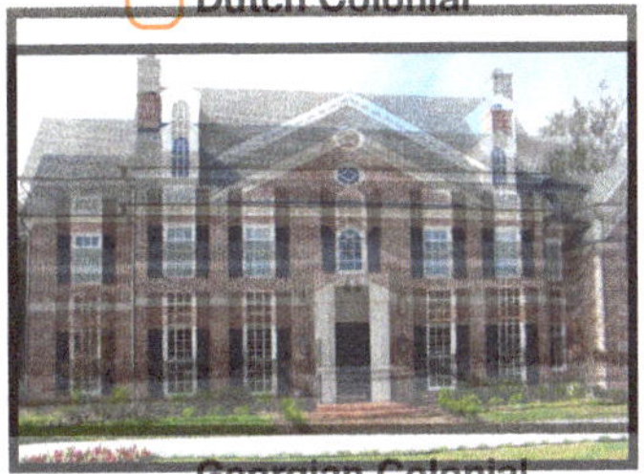
Georgian Colonial

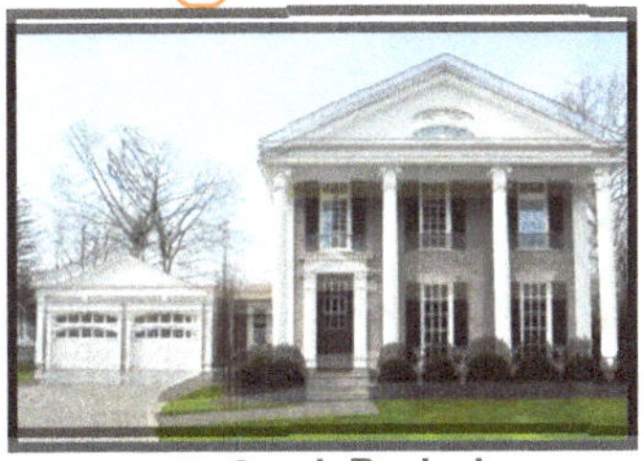
Greek Revival

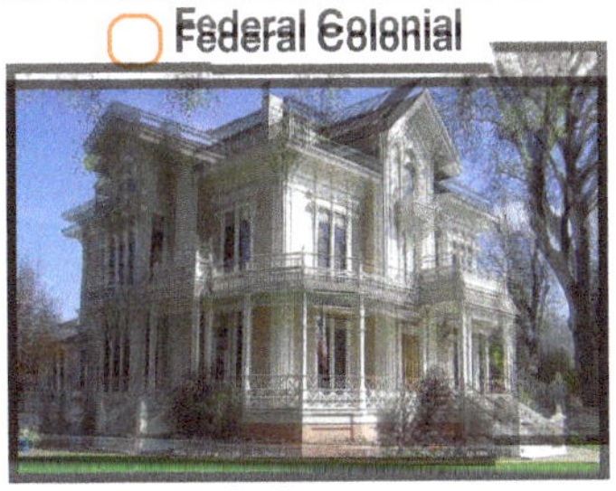
Italianate

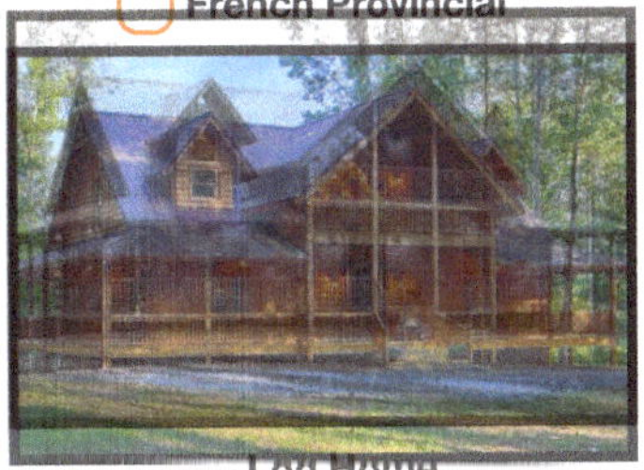
Log Home

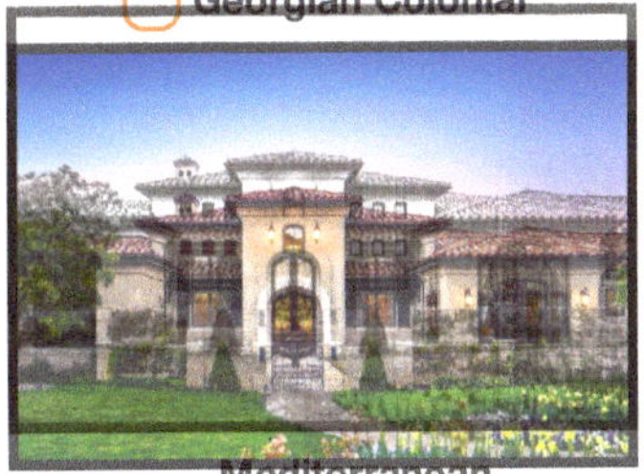
Mediterranean

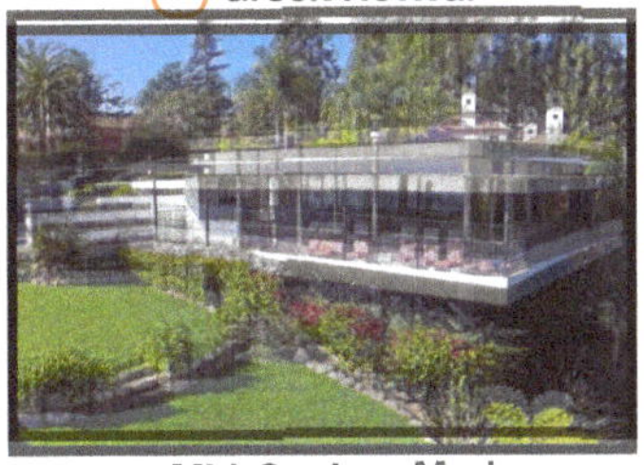
Mid-Century Modern

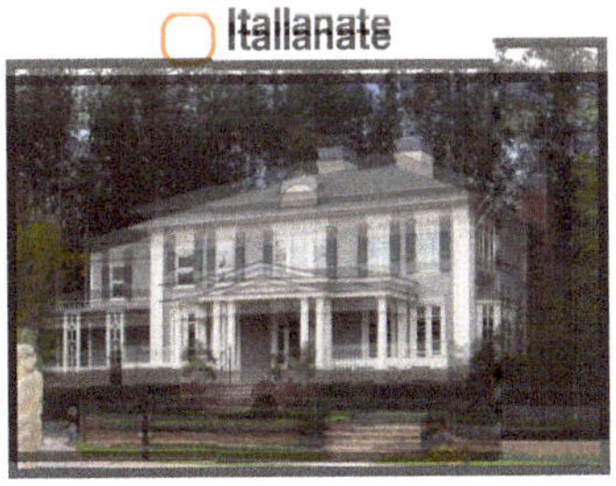
Neoclassical

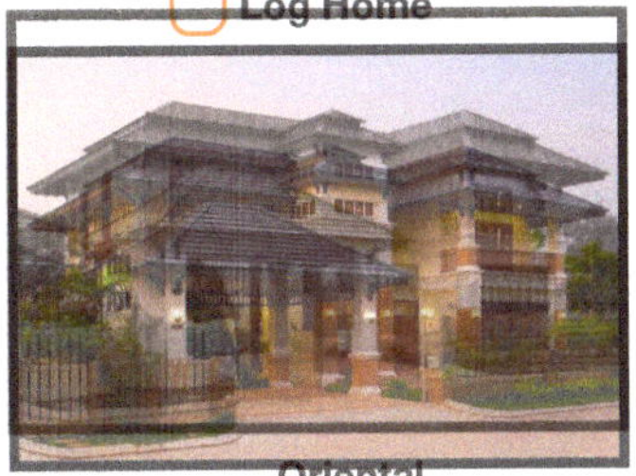
Oriental

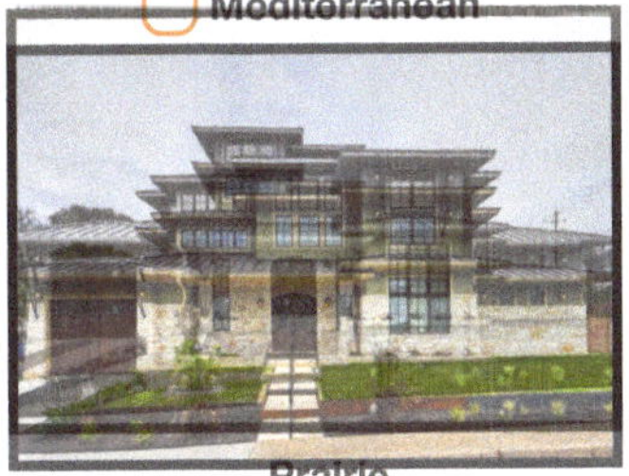
Prairie

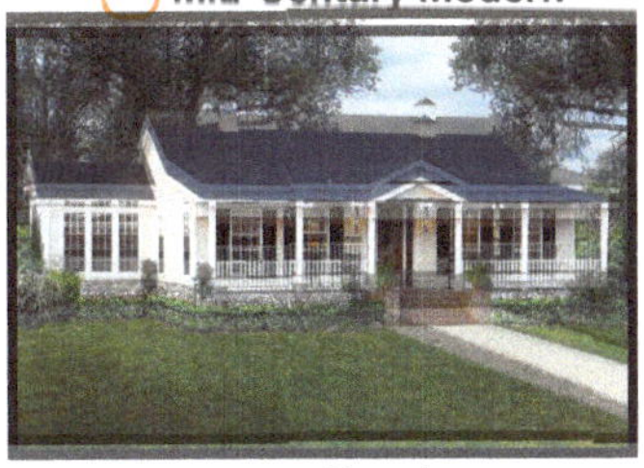
Ranch

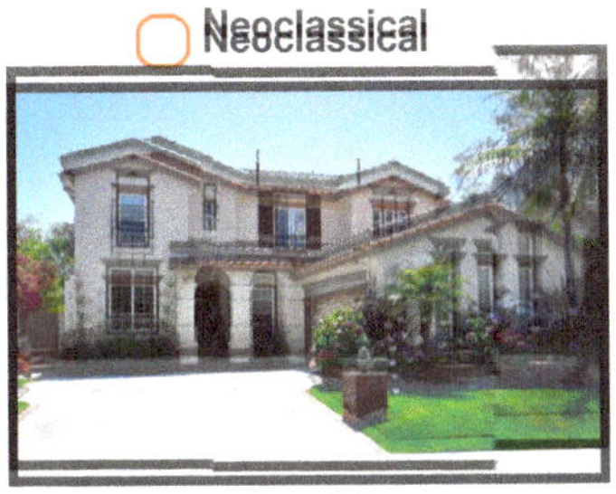
Spanish

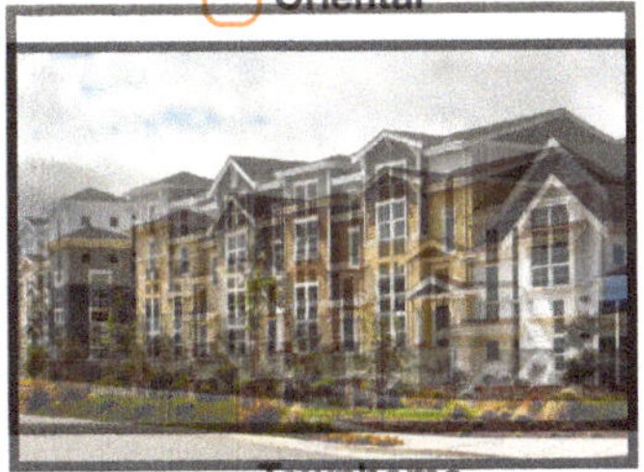
Townhome

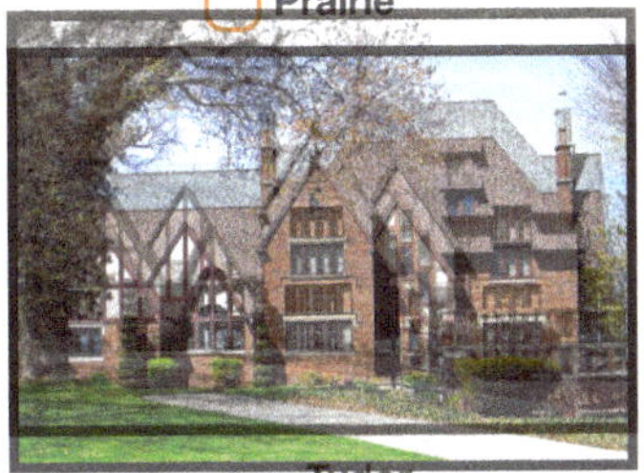
Tudor

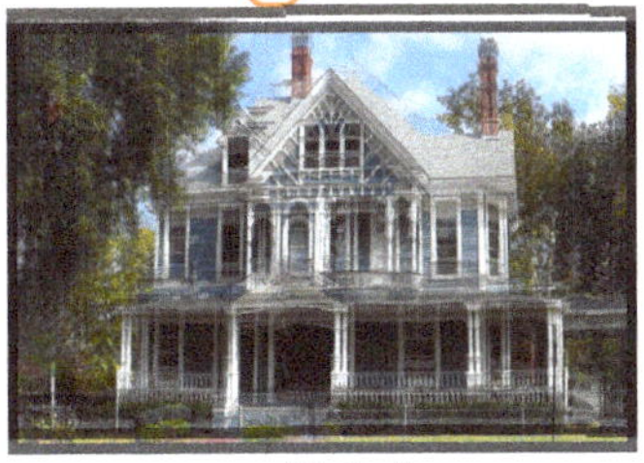
Victorian

YOUR TOP 3 PICKS:

©The Home Hunters Playbook

Individual home evaluation

Rate each property you visit (0= N/A, 1 = replace, 2 = repair, 3 = good, 4 = like, 5 = love)

Property Address: _____
_____
Builder/Architect: _____
# of Owners: _____ Year Built: _____
# of Bedrooms: _____ Sq Feet: _____
# of Bathrooms: _____ Lot Size: _____

Listing Price: _____
Mortgage/Rent: _____
Taxes: _____
HOA Fees: _____
Utilities: _____
Total Monthly: _____

Exterior Features and Condition

	0	1	2	3	4	5
Landscaping	○	○	○	○	○	○
Foundation	○	○	○	○	○	○
Paint	○	○	○	○	○	○
Windows	○	○	○	○	○	○
Roof/Gutters	○	○	○	○	○	○
Lighting	○	○	○	○	○	○
Fencing	○	○	○	○	○	○
Doors	○	○	○	○	○	○
Patio/Porch	○	○	○	○	○	○
Driveway	○	○	○	○	○	○
Chimney	○	○	○	○	○	○
Yard	○	○	○	○	○	○
Overall	○	○	○	○	○	○

Interior Features and Condition

	0	1	2	3	4	5
Kitchen	○	○	○	○	○	○
Bathrooms	○	○	○	○	○	○
Living Room	○	○	○	○	○	○
Floors	○	○	○	○	○	○
Basement	○	○	○	○	○	○
Attic	○	○	○	○	○	○
Closets	○	○	○	○	○	○
Walls	○	○	○	○	○	○
Ceilings	○	○	○	○	○	○
Lighting	○	○	○	○	○	○
Laundry	○	○	○	○	○	○
Appliances	○	○	○	○	○	○
Overall	○	○	○	○	○	○

Community Features and Condition

Location	○	○	○	○	○	○
Commute	○	○	○	○	○	○
Schools	○	○	○	○	○	○
Amenities	○	○	○	○	○	○
Things To Do	○	○	○	○	○	○
Shopping	○	○	○	○	○	○
Security	○	○	○	○	○	○

Systems and Extras

Electrical	○	○	○	○	○	○
Plumbing	○	○	○	○	○	○
Heating/AC	○	○	○	○	○	○
Pool/Hot Tub	○	○	○	○	○	○
Security	○	○	○	○	○	○
Cell Service	○	○	○	○	○	○
Fireplace	○	○	○	○	○	○

PROS:

CONS:

Individual home evaluation

Rate each property you visit (0= N/A, 1 = replace, 2 = repair, 3 = good, 4 = like, 5 = love)

Property Address: _____
_____
Builder/Architect: _____
# of Owners: _____   Year Built: _____
# of Bedrooms: _____   Sq Feet: _____
# of Bathrooms: _____   Lot Size: _____

Listing Price: _____
Mortgage/Rent: _____
Taxes: _____
HOA Fees: _____
Utilities: _____
Total Monthly: _____

Exterior Features and Condition

	0	1	2	3	4	5
Landscaping	○	○	○	○	○	○
Foundation	○	○	○	○	○	○
Paint	○	○	○	○	○	○
Windows	○	○	○	○	○	○
Roof/Gutters	○	○	○	○	○	○
Lighting	○	○	○	○	○	○
Fencing	○	○	○	○	○	○
Doors	○	○	○	○	○	○
Patio/Porch	○	○	○	○	○	○
Driveway	○	○	○	○	○	○
Chimney	○	○	○	○	○	○
Yard	○	○	○	○	○	○
Overall	○	○	○	○	○	○

Interior Features and Condition

	0	1	2	3	4	5
Kitchen	○	○	○	○	○	○
Bathrooms	○	○	○	○	○	○
Living Room	○	○	○	○	○	○
Floors	○	○	○	○	○	○
Basement	○	○	○	○	○	○
Attic	○	○	○	○	○	○
Closets	○	○	○	○	○	○
Walls	○	○	○	○	○	○
Ceilings	○	○	○	○	○	○
Lighting	○	○	○	○	○	○
Laundry	○	○	○	○	○	○
Appliances	○	○	○	○	○	○
Overall	○	○	○	○	○	○

Community Features and Condition

	0	1	2	3	4	5
Location	○	○	○	○	○	○
Commute	○	○	○	○	○	○
Schools	○	○	○	○	○	○
Amenities	○	○	○	○	○	○
Things To Do	○	○	○	○	○	○
Shopping	○	○	○	○	○	○
Security	○	○	○	○	○	○

Systems and Extras

	0	1	2	3	4	5
Electrical	○	○	○	○	○	○
Plumbing	○	○	○	○	○	○
Heating/AC	○	○	○	○	○	○
Pool/Hot Tub	○	○	○	○	○	○
Security	○	○	○	○	○	○
Cell Service	○	○	○	○	○	○
Fireplace	○	○	○	○	○	○

PROS:

CONS:

©The Home Hunters Playbook

Individual home evaluation

Rate each property you visit (0= N/A, 1 = replace, 2 = repair, 3 = good, 4 = like, 5 = love)

Property Address: _____
_____
Builder/Architect: _____
# of Owners: ____ Year Built: ____
# of Bedrooms: ____ Sq Feet: ____
# of Bathrooms: ____ Lot Size: ____

Listing Price: _____
Mortgage/Rent: _____
Taxes: _____
HOA Fees: _____
Utilities: _____
Total Monthly: _____

Exterior Features and Condition

	0	1	2	3	4	5
Landscaping	○	○	○	○	○	○
Foundation	○	○	○	○	○	○
Paint	○	○	○	○	○	○
Windows	○	○	○	○	○	○
Roof/Gutters	○	○	○	○	○	○
Lighting	○	○	○	○	○	○
Fencing	○	○	○	○	○	○
Doors	○	○	○	○	○	○
Patio/Porch	○	○	○	○	○	○
Driveway	○	○	○	○	○	○
Chimney	○	○	○	○	○	○
Yard	○	○	○	○	○	○
Overall	○	○	○	○	○	○

Interior Features and Condition

	0	1	2	3	4	5
Kitchen	○	○	○	○	○	○
Bathrooms	○	○	○	○	○	○
Living Room	○	○	○	○	○	○
Floors	○	○	○	○	○	○
Basement	○	○	○	○	○	○
Attic	○	○	○	○	○	○
Closets	○	○	○	○	○	○
Walls	○	○	○	○	○	○
Ceilings	○	○	○	○	○	○
Lighting	○	○	○	○	○	○
Laundry	○	○	○	○	○	○
Appliances	○	○	○	○	○	○
Overall	○	○	○	○	○	○

Community Features and Condition

	0	1	2	3	4	5
Location	○	○	○	○	○	○
Commute	○	○	○	○	○	○
Schools	○	○	○	○	○	○
Amenities	○	○	○	○	○	○
Things To Do	○	○	○	○	○	○
Shopping	○	○	○	○	○	○
Security	○	○	○	○	○	○

Systems and Extras

	0	1	2	3	4	5
Electrical	○	○	○	○	○	○
Plumbing	○	○	○	○	○	○
Heating/AC	○	○	○	○	○	○
Pool/Hot Tub	○	○	○	○	○	○
Security	○	○	○	○	○	○
Cell Service	○	○	○	○	○	○
Fireplace	○	○	○	○	○	○

PROS:

CONS:

©The Home Hunters Playbook

Individual home evaluation

Rate each property you visit (0= N/A, 1 = replace, 2 = repair, 3 = good, 4 = like, 5 = love)

Property Address: _____ Listing Price: _____
                   _____ Mortgage/Rent: _____
Builder/Architect: _____ Taxes: _____
# of Owners: _____ Year Built: _____ HOA Fees: _____
# of Bedrooms: ____ Sq Feet: _____   Utilities: _____
# of Bathrooms: ___ Lot Size: _____   Total Monthly: _____

Exterior Features and Condition

	0	1	2	3	4	5
Landscaping	○	○	○	○	○	○
Foundation	○	○	○	○	○	○
Paint	○	○	○	○	○	○
Windows	○	○	○	○	○	○
Roof/Gutters	○	○	○	○	○	○
Lighting	○	○	○	○	○	○
Fencing	○	○	○	○	○	○
Doors	○	○	○	○	○	○
Patio/Porch	○	○	○	○	○	○
Driveway	○	○	○	○	○	○
Chimney	○	○	○	○	○	○
Yard	○	○	○	○	○	○
Overall	○	○	○	○	○	○

Interior Features and Condition

	0	1	2	3	4	5
Kitchen	○	○	○	○	○	○
Bathrooms	○	○	○	○	○	○
Living Room	○	○	○	○	○	○
Floors	○	○	○	○	○	○
Basement	○	○	○	○	○	○
Attic	○	○	○	○	○	○
Closets	○	○	○	○	○	○
Walls	○	○	○	○	○	○
Ceilings	○	○	○	○	○	○
Lighting	○	○	○	○	○	○
Laundry	○	○	○	○	○	○
Appliances	○	○	○	○	○	○
Overall	○	○	○	○	○	○

Community Features and Condition

	0	1	2	3	4	5
Location	○	○	○	○	○	○
Commute	○	○	○	○	○	○
Schools	○	○	○	○	○	○
Amenities	○	○	○	○	○	○
Things To Do	○	○	○	○	○	○
Shopping	○	○	○	○	○	○
Security	○	○	○	○	○	○

Systems and Extras

	0	1	2	3	4	5
Electrical	○	○	○	○	○	○
Plumbing	○	○	○	○	○	○
Heating/AC	○	○	○	○	○	○
Pool/Hot Tub	○	○	○	○	○	○
Security	○	○	○	○	○	○
Cell Service	○	○	○	○	○	○
Fireplace	○	○	○	○	○	○

PROS:

CONS:

©The Home Hunters Playbook

Individual home evaluation

Rate each property you visit (0= N/A, 1 = replace, 2 = repair, 3 = good, 4 = like, 5 = love)

Property Address: _____

_____

Builder/Architect: _____

# of Owners: _____   Year Built: _____

# of Bedrooms: _____   Sq Feet: _____

# of Bathrooms: _____   Lot Size: _____

Listing Price: _____

Mortgage/Rent: _____

Taxes: _____

HOA Fees: _____

Utilities: _____

Total Monthly: _____

Exterior Features and Condition

	0	1	2	3	4	5
Landscaping	○	○	○	○	○	○
Foundation	○	○	○	○	○	○
Paint	○	○	○	○	○	○
Windows	○	○	○	○	○	○
Roof/Gutters	○	○	○	○	○	○
Lighting	○	○	○	○	○	○
Fencing	○	○	○	○	○	○
Doors	○	○	○	○	○	○
Patio/Porch	○	○	○	○	○	○
Driveway	○	○	○	○	○	○
Chimney	○	○	○	○	○	○
Yard	○	○	○	○	○	○
Overall	○	○	○	○	○	○

Interior Features and Condition

	0	1	2	3	4	5
Kitchen	○	○	○	○	○	○
Bathrooms	○	○	○	○	○	○
Living Room	○	○	○	○	○	○
Floors	○	○	○	○	○	○
Basement	○	○	○	○	○	○
Attic	○	○	○	○	○	○
Closets	○	○	○	○	○	○
Walls	○	○	○	○	○	○
Ceilings	○	○	○	○	○	○
Lighting	○	○	○	○	○	○
Laundry	○	○	○	○	○	○
Appliances	○	○	○	○	○	○
Overall	○	○	○	○	○	○

Community Features and Condition

Location	○	○	○	○	○	○
Commute	○	○	○	○	○	○
Schools	○	○	○	○	○	○
Amenities	○	○	○	○	○	○
Things To Do	○	○	○	○	○	○
Shopping	○	○	○	○	○	○
Security	○	○	○	○	○	○

Systems and Extras

Electrical	○	○	○	○	○	○
Plumbing	○	○	○	○	○	○
Heating/AC	○	○	○	○	○	○
Pool/Hot Tub	○	○	○	○	○	○
Security	○	○	○	○	○	○
Cell Service	○	○	○	○	○	○
Fireplace	○	○	○	○	○	○

PROS:

CONS:

©The Home Hunters Playbook

Individual home evaluation

Rate each property you visit (0= N/A, 1 = replace, 2 = repair, 3 = good, 4 = like, 5 = love)

Property Address: _____
_____
Builder/Architect: _____
# of Owners: _____   Year Built: _____
# of Bedrooms: _____   Sq Feet: _____
# of Bathrooms: _____   Lot Size: _____

Listing Price: _____
Mortgage/Rent: _____
Taxes: _____
HOA Fees: _____
Utilities: _____
Total Monthly: _____

Exterior Features and Condition

	0	1	2	3	4	5
Landscaping	○	○	○	○	○	○
Foundation	○	○	○	○	○	○
Paint	○	○	○	○	○	○
Windows	○	○	○	○	○	○
Roof/Gutters	○	○	○	○	○	○
Lighting	○	○	○	○	○	○
Fencing	○	○	○	○	○	○
Doors	○	○	○	○	○	○
Patio/Porch	○	○	○	○	○	○
Driveway	○	○	○	○	○	○
Chimney	○	○	○	○	○	○
Yard	○	○	○	○	○	○
Overall	○	○	○	○	○	○

Interior Features and Condition

	0	1	2	3	4	5
Kitchen	○	○	○	○	○	○
Bathrooms	○	○	○	○	○	○
Living Room	○	○	○	○	○	○
Floors	○	○	○	○	○	○
Basement	○	○	○	○	○	○
Attic	○	○	○	○	○	○
Closets	○	○	○	○	○	○
Walls	○	○	○	○	○	○
Ceilings	○	○	○	○	○	○
Lighting	○	○	○	○	○	○
Laundry	○	○	○	○	○	○
Appliances	○	○	○	○	○	○
Overall	○	○	○	○	○	○

Community Features and Condition

Location	○	○	○	○	○	○
Commute	○	○	○	○	○	○
Schools	○	○	○	○	○	○
Amenities	○	○	○	○	○	○
Things To Do	○	○	○	○	○	○
Shopping	○	○	○	○	○	○
Security	○	○	○	○	○	○

Systems and Extras

Electrical	○	○	○	○	○	○
Plumbing	○	○	○	○	○	○
Heating/AC	○	○	○	○	○	○
Pool/Hot Tub	○	○	○	○	○	○
Security	○	○	○	○	○	○
Cell Service	○	○	○	○	○	○
Fireplace	○	○	○	○	○	○

PROS:

CONS:

©The Home Hunters Playbook

Individual home evaluation

Rate each property you visit (0= N/A, 1 = replace, 2 = repair, 3 = good, 4 = like, 5 = love)

 PREP

Property Address: _____

_____

Builder/Architect: _____

# of Owners: _____   Year Built: _____

# of Bedrooms: _____   Sq Feet: _____

# of Bathrooms: _____   Lot Size: _____

Listing Price: _____

Mortgage/Rent: _____

Taxes: _____

HOA Fees: _____

Utilities: _____

Total Monthly: _____

Exterior Features and Condition

	0	1	2	3	4	5
Landscaping	○	○	○	○	○	○
Foundation	○	○	○	○	○	○
Paint	○	○	○	○	○	○
Windows	○	○	○	○	○	○
Roof/Gutters	○	○	○	○	○	○
Lighting	○	○	○	○	○	○
Fencing	○	○	○	○	○	○
Doors	○	○	○	○	○	○
Patio/Porch	○	○	○	○	○	○
Driveway	○	○	○	○	○	○
Chimney	○	○	○	○	○	○
Yard	○	○	○	○	○	○
Overall	○	○	○	○	○	○

Interior Features and Condition

	0	1	2	3	4	5
Kitchen	○	○	○	○	○	○
Bathrooms	○	○	○	○	○	○
Living Room	○	○	○	○	○	○
Floors	○	○	○	○	○	○
Basement	○	○	○	○	○	○
Attic	○	○	○	○	○	○
Closets	○	○	○	○	○	○
Walls	○	○	○	○	○	○
Ceilings	○	○	○	○	○	○
Lighting	○	○	○	○	○	○
Laundry	○	○	○	○	○	○
Appliances	○	○	○	○	○	○
Overall	○	○	○	○	○	○

Community Features and Condition

Location	○	○	○	○	○	○
Commute	○	○	○	○	○	○
Schools	○	○	○	○	○	○
Amenities	○	○	○	○	○	○
Things To Do	○	○	○	○	○	○
Shopping	○	○	○	○	○	○
Security	○	○	○	○	○	○

Systems and Extras

Electrical	○	○	○	○	○	○
Plumbing	○	○	○	○	○	○
Heating/AC	○	○	○	○	○	○
Pool/Hot Tub	○	○	○	○	○	○
Security	○	○	○	○	○	○
Cell Service	○	○	○	○	○	○
Fireplace	○	○	○	○	○	○

PROS:

CONS:

Individual home evaluation

Rate each property you visit (0= N/A, 1 = replace, 2 = repair, 3 = good, 4 = like, 5 = love)

Property Address:

Builder/Architect:

# of Owners:

# of Bedrooms:

# of Bathrooms:

Year Built:

Sq Feet:

Lot Size:

Listing Price:

Mortgage/Rent:

Taxes:

HOA Fees:

Utilities:

Total Monthly:

Exterior Features and Condition

	0	1	2	3	4	5
Landscaping	○	○	○	○	○	○
Foundation	○	○	○	○	○	○
Paint	○	○	○	○	○	○
Windows	○	○	○	○	○	○
Roof/Gutters	○	○	○	○	○	○
Lighting	○	○	○	○	○	○
Fencing	○	○	○	○	○	○
Doors	○	○	○	○	○	○
Patio/Porch	○	○	○	○	○	○
Driveway	○	○	○	○	○	○
Chimney	○	○	○	○	○	○
Yard	○	○	○	○	○	○
Overall	○	○	○	○	○	○

Interior Features and Condition

	0	1	2	3	4	5
Kitchen	○	○	○	○	○	○
Bathrooms	○	○	○	○	○	○
Living Room	○	○	○	○	○	○
Floors	○	○	○	○	○	○
Basement	○	○	○	○	○	○
Attic	○	○	○	○	○	○
Closets	○	○	○	○	○	○
Walls	○	○	○	○	○	○
Ceilings	○	○	○	○	○	○
Lighting	○	○	○	○	○	○
Laundry	○	○	○	○	○	○
Appliances	○	○	○	○	○	○
Overall	○	○	○	○	○	○

Community Features and Condition

	0	1	2	3	4	5
Location	○	○	○	○	○	○
Commute	○	○	○	○	○	○
Schools	○	○	○	○	○	○
Amenities	○	○	○	○	○	○
Things To Do	○	○	○	○	○	○
Shopping	○	○	○	○	○	○
Security	○	○	○	○	○	○

Systems and Extras

	0	1	2	3	4	5
Electrical	○	○	○	○	○	○
Plumbing	○	○	○	○	○	○
Heating/AC	○	○	○	○	○	○
Pool/Hot Tub	○	○	○	○	○	○
Security	○	○	○	○	○	○
Cell Service	○	○	○	○	○	○
Fireplace	○	○	○	○	○	○

PROS:

CONS:

©The Home Hunters Playbook

Individual home evaluation

Rate each property you visit (0= N/A, 1 = replace, 2 = repair, 3 = good, 4 = like, 5 = love)

Property Address: _____
_____
Builder/Architect: _____
# of Owners: _____ Year Built: _____
# of Bedrooms: _____ Sq Feet: _____
# of Bathrooms: _____ Lot Size: _____

Listing Price: _____
Mortgage/Rent: _____
Taxes: _____
HOA Fees: _____
Utilities: _____
Total Monthly: _____

Exterior Features and Condition

	0	1	2	3	4	5
Landscaping	○	○	○	○	○	○
Foundation	○	○	○	○	○	○
Paint	○	○	○	○	○	○
Windows	○	○	○	○	○	○
Roof/Gutters	○	○	○	○	○	○
Lighting	○	○	○	○	○	○
Fencing	○	○	○	○	○	○
Doors	○	○	○	○	○	○
Patio/Porch	○	○	○	○	○	○
Driveway	○	○	○	○	○	○
Chimney	○	○	○	○	○	○
Yard	○	○	○	○	○	○
Overall	○	○	○	○	○	○

Interior Features and Condition

	0	1	2	3	4	5
Kitchen	○	○	○	○	○	○
Bathrooms	○	○	○	○	○	○
Living Room	○	○	○	○	○	○
Floors	○	○	○	○	○	○
Basement	○	○	○	○	○	○
Attic	○	○	○	○	○	○
Closets	○	○	○	○	○	○
Walls	○	○	○	○	○	○
Ceilings	○	○	○	○	○	○
Lighting	○	○	○	○	○	○
Laundry	○	○	○	○	○	○
Appliances	○	○	○	○	○	○
Overall	○	○	○	○	○	○

Community Features and Condition

	0	1	2	3	4	5
Location	○	○	○	○	○	○
Commute	○	○	○	○	○	○
Schools	○	○	○	○	○	○
Amenities	○	○	○	○	○	○
Things To Do	○	○	○	○	○	○
Shopping	○	○	○	○	○	○
Security	○	○	○	○	○	○

Systems and Extras

	0	1	2	3	4	5
Electrical	○	○	○	○	○	○
Plumbing	○	○	○	○	○	○
Heating/AC	○	○	○	○	○	○
Pool/Hot Tub	○	○	○	○	○	○
Security	○	○	○	○	○	○
Cell Service	○	○	○	○	○	○
Fireplace	○	○	○	○	○	○

PROS:

CONS:

©The Home Hunters Playbook

Individual home evaluation

Rate each property you visit (0= N/A, 1 = replace, 2 = repair, 3 = good, 4 = like, 5 = love)

Property Address: _____
_____
Builder/Architect: _____
# of Owners: _____ Year Built: _____
# of Bedrooms: _____ Sq Feet: _____
# of Bathrooms: _____ Lot Size: _____

Listing Price: _____
Mortgage/Rent: _____
Taxes: _____
HOA Fees: _____
Utilities: _____
Total Monthly: _____

Exterior Features and Condition

	0	1	2	3	4	5
Landscaping	○	○	○	○	○	○
Foundation	○	○	○	○	○	○
Paint	○	○	○	○	○	○
Windows	○	○	○	○	○	○
Roof/Gutters	○	○	○	○	○	○
Lighting	○	○	○	○	○	○
Fencing	○	○	○	○	○	○
Doors	○	○	○	○	○	○
Patio/Porch	○	○	○	○	○	○
Driveway	○	○	○	○	○	○
Chimney	○	○	○	○	○	○
Yard	○	○	○	○	○	○
Overall	○	○	○	○	○	○

Interior Features and Condition

	0	1	2	3	4	5
Kitchen	○	○	○	○	○	○
Bathrooms	○	○	○	○	○	○
Living Room	○	○	○	○	○	○
Floors	○	○	○	○	○	○
Basement	○	○	○	○	○	○
Attic	○	○	○	○	○	○
Closets	○	○	○	○	○	○
Walls	○	○	○	○	○	○
Ceilings	○	○	○	○	○	○
Lighting	○	○	○	○	○	○
Laundry	○	○	○	○	○	○
Appliances	○	○	○	○	○	○
Overall	○	○	○	○	○	○

Community Features and Condition

	0	1	2	3	4	5
Location	○	○	○	○	○	○
Commute	○	○	○	○	○	○
Schools	○	○	○	○	○	○
Amenities	○	○	○	○	○	○
Things To Do	○	○	○	○	○	○
Shopping	○	○	○	○	○	○
Security	○	○	○	○	○	○

Systems and Extras

	0	1	2	3	4	5
Electrical	○	○	○	○	○	○
Plumbing	○	○	○	○	○	○
Heating/AC	○	○	○	○	○	○
Pool/Hot Tub	○	○	○	○	○	○
Security	○	○	○	○	○	○
Cell Service	○	○	○	○	○	○
Fireplace	○	○	○	○	○	○

PROS:

CONS:

©The Home Hunters Playbook

MOVE
notes

Moving timeline checklist
Use this to plan your move from 2 months out through moving day!

2 MONTHS OUT

- Acquire estimates from at least 3 moving companies
- Create and maintain a file for all moving papers and receipts (potential tax deductions)
- Check with your insurance providers to see what could be covered during your move.
- Organize your possessions and sell, donate or give things away you don't want to move with.
- Take photos of shelves, drawers or closets you want to set up the same in your new home.
- If moving from a rental property get a copy of the inspection checklist so you know what needs to be fixed or cleaned prior to leaving.

6 WEEKS OUT

- Start using the **Change of Address Checklist** in this Playbook to start notifying everyone of your upcoming move.
- Find new doctors for your family's needs in the area and have your medical records transferred to them (primary, specialists, veterinarian, etc.)
- Arrange to have your children's school records transferred.
- Select your moving company or reserve a rental truck for your moving day - check on insurance, mileage included and return times.
- Paint over any scuff marks or revert back to previous colors.
- Remove any nails, hangings or mounted TVs and cover up any holes.

30 DAYS OUT

- Arrange for moving day travel such as air, hotel, car rental.
- Reserve transportation of pets, plants, food and other delicate or perishable items.
- Contact all current utilities to arrange final billing and disconnection dates.
- Contact utilities at your new home and arrange connection dates and any payments due before you move in (like electric and water!)
- Contact insurance companies to arrange coverage at your new address:
  - Auto ◯ Home ◯ Medical
- Have a preliminary inspection from your landlord to be sure you have completed any repairs required before moving day.

30 DAYS OUT (CON'T)

- Make arrangements for any repair or cleaning that is required before moving out.
- Gather all legal and important documents in one box that is easily accessible during your move in case you need them:
  - Vehicle Titles ◯ Wills
  - Vehicle Registrations ◯ Deeds
  - Vehicle Insurances ◯ Stocks
  - Social Security Cards ◯ Passports
  - Birth Certificates ◯ Medical
- Check to make sure your current bank is near your new home and open a new account if neccessary, then transfer funds.
- Request refunds on unused renters/homeowner's insurances or prepaid services from your current area.
- Purchase moving supplies such as boxes, bubble wrap, tape, markers, rope, etc. Ask friends or stores in the area to save money!
- Request and schedule time off from work or make arrangements with your business for when you will be moving
- **START PACKING!!!**

2-3 WEEKS OUT

- Arrange for child or pet care on moving day
- Complete the **Change of Address Checklist** in this playbook and make sure everyone knows about your upcoming move!
- Review arrangements with your moving company to make sure all dates and information is correct.
- If planning on a long trip or moving with your personal vehicles schedule a service checkup.

7 DAYS OUT

- Drain gas and oil from any power equipment you'll be moving (mower, weed wacker, etc.)
- Make sure all prescriptions are filled
- Label your boxes and use the **Moving Box Inventory** list to track where and what is in each one for easy unpacking.
- Return anything you've borrowed or rented from friends, relatives or vendors in the area.

©The Home Hunters Playbook

3 DAYS OUT

- Defrost refrigerators and freezers
- Complete final load of laundry
- Pack first night items such as: change of clothes, flashlight, phone, sheets, toiletries, cell phone charger, computer/charger
- Build a Moving Survival Kit:
  - Snacks & drinks for the trip
  - Extra cash for emergencies
  - Pain relievers (aspirin/tylenol)
  - Medical (band aids, ointments, etc.
  - Paper cups, plates, utensils
  - Paper towels, toilet paper, soap
  - Garbage bags
  - Pad and Paper
  - Scissors/Utility Knife
  - Tape, Rope, Bungee Cords
  - Medications, prescriptions, vitamins
- Conduct a final cleaning of your entire space and keep some supplies unpacked for any messes that may happen during the move:

MOVING DAY

- Organize boxes/furniture by room so it is easy to move and unpack
- Be home at ALL TIMES to answer any questions if hiring movers
- Record all utility readings for accurate billing
- Check EVERY room THREE times before leaving the home for anything that could have been left behind
- Take out all remaining trash and recycling

NOTES

29

Change of address checklist
Keep track of your change of addresses and new utility connections

UTILITIES

- ◯ **Electricity**
  - Date of Cancellation: ▢
  - New Connection Date: ▢
- ◯ **Gas**
  - Date of Cancellation: ▢
  - New Connection Date: ▢
- ◯ **Water**
  - Date of Cancellation: ▢
  - New Connection Date: ▢
- ◯ **Cable/Internet/Phone**
  - Date of Cancellation: ▢
  - New Connection Date: ▢
- ◯ **Trash / Recycling**
  - New Trash Pickup: ▢
  - New Recycling Pickup: ▢
- ◯ **Mobile Phone**

FINANCIAL

- ◯ **Employment (HR/Payroll)**
- ◯ **Banks**
- ◯ **Credit Cards / Virtual Payment (PayPal)**
- ◯ **Loans (Auto, Student, Personal, etc)**
- ◯ **Insurances**
  - ◯ Auto ◯ Medical ◯ Life ◯ Home/Renters
- ◯ **Investments/Brokerage**

GOVERNMENT

- ◯ **Social Security**
- ◯ **Department of Motor Vehicles**
  - ◯ License ◯ Registration
- ◯ **US Postal Office Forwarding**
- ◯ **Voter Registration**

MEMBERSHIPS

- ◯ **Professional Associations**
- ◯ **Gyms**
- ◯ **Churches**
- ◯ **Country Clubs**
- ◯ **Alma Maters**
- ◯ **Non-Profit Organizations**
- ◯ **Extracurricular Activities**
- ◯ **Licensing Boards**
- ◯ **Civic Organizations**
- ◯ **Magazine/Subscriptions**
- ◯ **Community Groups**

SERVICES

- ◯ **Home**
  - ◯ Housekeeping ◯ Delivery ◯ Landscaping
- ◯ **Childcare**
  - ◯ School ◯ Daycare ◯ Babysitter ◯ Carpool
- ◯ **Entertainment** (online streaming services)
- ◯ **Doctors**
- ◯ **Lawyers**
- ◯ **Accountants**
- ◯ **Pets**
  - ◯ Vet ◯ Groomer ◯ Walker/Sitter

OTHER

- ◯ **Family Notified**
- ◯ **Friends Notified**
- ◯ **Business Contacts Notified**
- ◯ **New Mailing Address Labels**

©The Home Hunters Playbook

Moving to do list
Use this to organize other "to dos" before or during your move!

TASK	PRIORITY LEVEL	DUE DATE	COMPLETED
	○ LOW ○ MEDIUM ○ HIGH	/	/
	○ LOW ○ MEDIUM ○ HIGH	/	/
	○ LOW ○ MEDIUM ○ HIGH	/	/
	○ LOW ○ MEDIUM ○ HIGH	/	/
	○ LOW ○ MEDIUM ○ HIGH	/	/
	○ LOW ○ MEDIUM ○ HIGH	/	/
	○ LOW ○ MEDIUM ○ HIGH	/	/
	○ LOW ○ MEDIUM ○ HIGH	/	/
	○ LOW ○ MEDIUM ○ HIGH	/	/
	○ LOW ○ MEDIUM ○ HIGH	/	/
	○ LOW ○ MEDIUM ○ HIGH	/	/
	○ LOW ○ MEDIUM ○ HIGH	/	/
	○ LOW ○ MEDIUM ○ HIGH	/	/
	○ LOW ○ MEDIUM ○ HIGH	/	/
	○ LOW ○ MEDIUM ○ HIGH	/	/
	○ LOW ○ MEDIUM ○ HIGH	/	/

©The Home Hunters Playbook

Things to sell, donate or give
Turn what you don't want into extra cash or give to a cause!

WHAT NEEDS A NEW HOME?		PRICE?	SOLD FOR?	NEW OWNER?
	○ SELL ○ DONATE ○ GIVE			
	○ SELL ○ DONATE ○ GIVE			
	○ SELL ○ DONATE ○ GIVE			
	○ SELL ○ DONATE ○ GIVE			
	○ SELL ○ DONATE ○ GIVE			
	○ SELL ○ DONATE ○ GIVE			
	○ SELL ○ DONATE ○ GIVE			
	○ SELL ○ DONATE ○ GIVE			
	○ SELL ○ DONATE ○ GIVE			
	○ SELL ○ DONATE ○ GIVE			
	○ SELL ○ DONATE ○ GIVE			
	○ SELL ○ DONATE ○ GIVE			
	○ SELL ○ DONATE ○ GIVE			

©The Home Hunters Playbook
©The Home Hunters Playbook

Moving box inventory
Use this to organize each box so it's easy to unpack at your new home!

BOX #	DESTINATION	CONTENTS

Needs for your home checklist
Use this list to make sure you have everything to make it your home!

ENTRANCE AREA
- ☐ Welcome Mat
- ☐ Front Porch Furniture/Seats
- ☐ Area Rug
- ☐ Area/Table/Hooks for keys
- ☐ Umbrella holder
- ☐ _____
- ☐ _____
- ☐ _____

LIVING ROOM
- ☐ Seating (couch, loveseat, chairs)
- ☐ Throw Pillows
- ☐ Throw Blanket
- ☐ Coffee Table
- ☐ Accent Tables
- ☐ Lamps
- ☐ Television
- ☐ Television Stand
- ☐ Artwork/Decorations
- ☐ Area Rug
- ☐ Coasters
- ☐ Vacuum / Steamer
- ☐ _____
- ☐ _____
- ☐ _____

KITCHEN/DINING
- ☐ Table with Chairs
- ☐ Dishes
- ☐ Silverware
- ☐ Silverware Organizer
- ☐ Knife Set
- ☐ Pots and Pans
- ☐ Mixing Bowls
- ☐ Measuring Cups and Spoons
- ☐ Cooking Utensils
- ☐ Storage Containers
- ☐ Oven mitts
- ☐ Trash Can and Bags
- ☐ Dish Drying Rack
- ☐ Toaster
- ☐ Blender
- ☐ Can Opener
- ☐ Colander
- ☐ Coffee Machine
- ☐ Tea Pot
- ☐ Food Processor
- ☐ Spices
- ☐ Cutting Boards
- ☐ Glasses and Mugs
- ☐ Wine/Bottle Opener
- ☐ _____
- ☐ _____
- ☐ _____

FOOD/GROCERIES
- ☐ Milk (dairy, almond, soy, coconut, etc.)
- ☐ Breads (or gluten free options)
- ☐ Eggs
- ☐ Cheeses (or dairy free options)
- ☐ Vegetables (only purchase weekly)
- ☐ Fruits (only purchase weekly)
- ☐ Meat (steak, chicken, pork, etc.)
- ☐ Seafood (fish, shrimp, crab, etc.)
- ☐ Cereal
- ☐ Pasta
- ☐ Rice
- ☐ Snacks (pretzels, chips, salsa, etc.)
- ☐ Baking (flour, sugar, pancake mix, etc.)
- ☐ Cooking (oils, vinegars, sauces, etc.)
- ☐ Frozen (meals, pizza, waffles, ice cream, etc.)
- ☐ Ziplock Bags
- ☐ Aluminum Foil
- ☐ Plastic Wrap
- ☐ Cleaning Supplies (all purpose, glass, etc.)
- ☐ Detergents (dishwasher, laundry)
- ☐ Toilet Paper and Paper Towels
- ☐ Sponges/ Dish Towels
- ☐ Toiletries (toothpaste, deodorant, soap, etc.)
- ☐ Pet Food/Supplies
- ☐ _____
- ☐ _____
- ☐ _____

BATHROOMS
- ☐ Towels
- ☐ Hand Towels
- ☐ Wash Cloths
- ☐ Bath Rugs
- ☐ Toilet Paper
- ☐ Deodorizer
- ☐ Plunger
- ☐ Shower Curtain
- ☐ Trash Can
- ☐ Hand Soap
- ☐ Toiletries
- ☐ _____
- ☐ _____
- ☐ _____

OUTDOOR AREAS
- ☐ Grill
- ☐ Fire pit
- ☐ Patio Furniture
- ☐ Flowers/Plants
- ☐ Mower
- ☐ Weedwacker
- ☐ Gardening Gloves
- ☐ Hedge Trimmers
- ☐ Extension Cord
- ☐ Large refuse/lawn bags
- ☐ Rake
- ☐ Bungee cords for trash cans

LAUNDRY
- ☐ Washer and Dryer
- ☐ Stain Remover
- ☐ Hangers
- ☐ Clothing Hamper
- ☐ Sewing Kit
- ☐ _____
- ☐ _____
- ☐ _____

NOTES:

©The Home Hunters Playbook

CLEAN
notes

Cleaning checklists
Use this to keep your home clean without feeling overwhelmed!

DAILY CLEANING LIST

- ☐ Make all beds
- ☐ Wash dishes / run dishwasher
- ☐ Scrub kitchen sink
- ☐ Wipe down countertops
- ☐ Wash kitchen table
- ☐ Sweep floors
- ☐ Complete 1 load of laundry
- ☐ Wipe down bathrooms
- ☐ Open mail and file papers
- ☐ Pick up toys, papers, laundry
- ☐ Take out garbage & recycling
- ☐ Vacuum main living areas

WEEKLY CLEANING LIST

- ☐ Water plants
- ☐ Wash door knobs
- ☐ Wipe all mirrors, glass, TVs
- ☐ Scrub toilets
- ☐ Vacuum all rooms/stairs
- ☐ Mop all hardwood floors
- ☐ Wash all towels
- ☐ Clean tubs/showers
- ☐ Wash sheets & pillowcases
- ☐ Wipe down appliances
- ☐ Clean out fridge
- ☐ Grocery shopping

MONTHLY CLEANING LIST

- ☐ Wipe down all doors
- ☐ Dust lamps/fans/shelves
- ☐ Vacuum and wipe baseboards
- ☐ Wipe all chair legs and tables
- ☐ Tidy up cupboards/pantry
- ☐ Deodorize throw pillows
- ☐ Wash throw blankets/quilts
- ☐ Clean out Freezer
- ☐ Wipe down cabinets
- ☐ Dust air vents/window sills
- ☐ Clean microwave and oven
- ☐ Sweep garage

SEMI ANNUAL CLEANING LIST

- ☐ Vacuum exhaust fans
- ☐ Vacuum behind/under furniture
- ☐ Wash rugs
- ☐ Launder throw pillows
- ☐ Launder comforters
- ☐ Wash decorative towels
- ☐ Dust tops of cabinets
- ☐ Spot clean walls
- ☐ Clean closets
- ☐ Sort/donate clothing
- ☐ Sweep all patios and decks
- ☐ Clean inside of all drawers

ANNUAL CLEANING LIST

- ☐ Launder curtains
- ☐ Wash all windows
- ☐ Vacuum behind fridge
- ☐ Vacuum behind washer/dryer
- ☐ Clean dryer vent
- ☐ Get carpets cleaned
- ☐ Clean fireplace
- ☐ Clean grill/fire pit
- ☐ Wash siding
- ☐ Wash patios and decks
- ☐ Tidy storeroom/attic
- ☐ Clean garage out

©The Home Hunters Playbook

36

Seasonal Maintenance checklist

Use this to keep your home maintained, clean and safe year round!

MONTHLY MAINTENANCE	JAN.	FEB.	MAR.	APR.	MAY	JUN.	JUL.	AUG.	SEPT.	OCT.	NOV.	DEC.
Inspect/Change HVAC filters	☐	☐	☐	☐	☐	☐	☐	☐	☐	☐	☐	☐
Test CO2 & smoke detectors	☐	☐	☐	☐	☐	☐	☐	☐	☐	☐	☐	☐
Rotate/flip mattresses/cushions	☐	☐	☐	☐	☐	☐	☐	☐	☐	☐	☐	☐
Inspect fire extinguishers	☐	☐	☐	☐	☐	☐	☐	☐	☐	☐	☐	☐
Clean garbage disposal	☐	☐	☐	☐	☐	☐	☐	☐	☐	☐	☐	☐
Test CO2 & smoke detectors	☐	☐	☐	☐	☐	☐	☐	☐	☐	☐	☐	☐
Clean microwave & oven	☐	☐	☐	☐	☐	☐	☐	☐	☐	☐	☐	☐

FALL (SEPT, OCT, NOV)

- ☐ Clean gutters
- ☐ Prepare storm windows/ hurricane kit
- ☐ Rake leaves & dispose of mulch
- ☐ Clean garage
- ☐ Check/Re-seal driveway
- ☐ Caulk any leaks in windows/doors
- ☐ Get chimney cleaned
- ☐ Clean out fireplace
- ☐ Flush hot water heater/remove sediment
- ☐ Clean refrigerator drip pan
- ☐ Get furnace inspected/repaired
- ☐ Fertilize and reseed lawn if necessary

SUMMER (JUN, JULY, AUG)

- ☐ Clean/repair deck or patio area
- ☐ Spray for ants, insects and wasps
- ☐ Prune trees & shrubs
- ☐ Flush out all interior drains
- ☐ Pour bleach/vinegar in A/C drain line
- ☐ Drain/flush water heater
- ☐ Clean range hood filter
- ☐ Replace batteries in smoke detectors
- ☐ Power wash exteriors, windows & siding
- ☐ Maintain yard growth
- ☐ Clean aerators on faucets
- ☐ Inspect roof and repair if necessary

SPRING (MAR, APR, MAY)

- ☐ Clean gutters
- ☐ Repair/replace window screens
- ☐ Have A/C serviced
- ☐ Touch up peeling/damaged paint
- ☐ Clear dead plants/shrubs
- ☐ Have trees trimmed by power lines
- ☐ Fertilize and reseed lawn if necessary
- ☐ Clean grill & patio furniture
- ☐ Flush hot water heater/remove sediment
- ☐ Add mulch to flower beds
- ☐ Power wash driveway, decks, patio area
- ☐ Clean the garage, basement & attic

WINTER (DEC, JAN & FEB)

- ☐ Tighten any handles, knobs, racks, etc.
- ☐ Conduct a Deep Clean
- ☐ Add weather stripping where needed
- ☐ Vacuum refrigerator coils
- ☐ Winterize A/C
- ☐ Winterize sprinkler system
- ☐ Inspect plumbing for leaks
- ☐ Flush outdoor water faucets & hoses
- ☐ Pour bleach/vinegar in A/C drain line
- ☐ Check for ice dams & icicles
- ☐ Clean showerheads
- ☐ Remove screens & install storm windows

©The Home Hunters Playbook

DEEP CLEAN checklist
Complete this 1-2 times per year so your home stays in great condition

ENTIRE HOUSEHOLD
- ☐ Organize closets
- ☐ Dust/clean all mirrors, frames & decorations
- ☐ Dust/vacuum all lamps and shades
- ☐ Remove all cobwebs
- ☐ Wash walls/ touch up paint
- ☐ Wash skirting boards, door frames and doors
- ☐ Dust light fixtures and fans
- ☐ Clean windows/blinds/screens and tracks
- ☐ Dust/wash or replace air vents if necessary
- ☐ Vacuum and shampoo all carpets
- ☐ Dust/shine overhead lights, replace bulbs
- ☐ Move all furniture to sweep/dust & vacuum
- ☐ Wash all curtains and blinds
- ☐ Dust/polish/wax all furniture

KITCHEN
- ☐ Wash cabinets/drawers/shelves - inside & out
- ☐ Clean and defrost freezer
- ☐ Deep clean oven/microwave/dishwasher
- ☐ Move stove - vacuum & mop behind it
- ☐ Vacuum stove vents
- ☐ Move fridge - vacuum & mop behind it
- ☐ Vacuum coils on fridge (unplug first)
- ☐ Clean food trap in dishwasher
- ☐ Clean fridge shelves, trays & doors
- ☐ Disinfect and shine sink
- ☐ Clean countertops & backsplashes
- ☐ Sweep, mop and wax floors
- ☐ Clean/purge cabinets, pantry & cupboards
- ☐ Wash/polish all silverware

LIVING ROOMS
- ☐ Clean television screen and other electronics
- ☐ Wash all pillows and blankets
- ☐ Wash/clean all upholstery and curtains
- ☐ Wax/dust/polish any furniture
- ☐ Vacuum couch crevices, fluff all pillows
- ☐ Clean our fireplace if necessary

BATHROOMS
- ☐ Remove scum using water, vinegar & lemon juice
- ☐ Get rid of toilet rings w/ swipe of dryer sheet
- ☐ Place bag w/vinegar on showerhead overnight
- ☐ Wipe faucets with dryer sheets for shine
- ☐ Wash/replace shower curtains/liners
- ☐ Clean all mirrors shower doors
- ☐ Wash all bathmats & towels
- ☐ Mop floors
- ☐ Clean toilets, countertops, tubs and showers
- ☐ Reorganize and clean under sink and cupboards
- ☐ Throw away unused or expired products
- ☐ Scrub and reseal tile grout
- ☐ Check/fix and leaks or clogs
- ☐ Wipe down exterior of drawers & cupboards

BEDROOMS
- ☐ Wash all bedding - skirt and duvet included
- ☐ Flip or rotate mattress
- ☐ Clean out closets, donate unused items
- ☐ Clean mattress by mixing baking soda/lavender oil. Spread over mattress, wait 1 hour and vacuum

OFFICE
- ☐ Dust/clean computer, keyboard, monitor
- ☐ Clean out/organize all drawers, cabinets & shelves
- ☐ Organize house paperwork & bills
- ☐ Shred old/unnecessary documents

UTILITY SPACE/ LAUNDRY AREA
- ☐ Run empty washing machine with bleach
- ☐ Sweep/mop under washing/dryer machines
- ☐ Vacuum out lint drawer
- ☐ Clean/organize attic & basement

OUTSIDE/ENTRY/PORCH
- ☐ Clean siding, doors and windows
- ☐ Scrub porch ceiling, walls, railings & floor
- ☐ Check for cracks and recaulk if necessary
- ☐ Clean/repair gutters, fixtures, furniture

©The Home Hunters Playbook

ORGANIZE
notes

Monthly Budget Worksheet

Use this to stay on top of your monthly income, expenses and goals!

INCOME:

Source:	Amount:		Item:	Cost:	Saved:	Needed:
		GOALS				

Total Income (+):
Total Expenses (-):
Monthly Total:

EXPENSES:
Such as: housing, utilities, credit cards, transportation, groceries, education, loans, savings, insurances, entertainment - anything that goes out

	budgeted	actual	difference	notes

TOTALS:

Password Keeper
Use this to organize your logins for websites & online accounts

WEBSITE	USERNAME	PASSWORD

Warranty Tracker
Use this to organize warranties for household items

Item Description:
Manufacturer Name:
Purchase Date:
Model Number:
Warranty Number:

Cost of Item:
Cost of Warranty:
Warranty Expiration:
Serial Number:
Phone Number:

Details/Notes:

Item Description:
Manufacturer Name:
Purchase Date:
Model Number:
Warranty Number:

Cost of Item:
Cost of Warranty:
Warranty Expiration:
Serial Number:
Phone Number:

Details/Notes:

Item Description:
Manufacturer Name:
Purchase Date:
Model Number:
Warranty Number:

Cost of Item:
Cost of Warranty:
Warranty Expiration:
Serial Number:
Phone Number:

Details/Notes:

Household Purchase Tracker

Keep your household purchases organized and in one place!

YOUR PURCHASE	FROM WHERE?	DATE	COST

©The Home Hunters Playbook

Maintenance Tracker

Use this to know what, when and by who helped maintain your home

Item for Maintenance:		Maintenance Date:
Maintenance reason:		Maintenance Cost:
Company:		Website:
Phone Number:		Email Address:
Details/Notes:		

Item for Maintenance:		Maintenance Date:
Maintenance reason:		Maintenance Cost:
Company:		Website:
Phone Number:		Email Address:
Details/Notes:		

Item for Maintenance:		Maintenance Date:
Maintenance reason:		Maintenance Cost:
Company:		Website:
Phone Number:		Email Address:
Details/Notes:		

Item for Maintenance:		Maintenance Date:
Maintenance reason:		Maintenance Cost:
Company:		Website:
Phone Number:		Email Address:
Details/Notes:		

©The Home Hunters Playbook

In Case of Emergency 9-1-1
Use this as a reference for emergency numbers and procedures

FIRE DEPARTMENT
Number: _____
Address: _____
_____
Distance from home: _____

POLICE DEPARTMENT
Number: _____
Address: _____
_____
Distance from home: _____

NEAREST HOSPITAL
Number: _____
Address: _____
_____
Distance from home: _____

Primary Care Physician
Name: _____
Phone: _____
Address: _____

Closest Emergency Contact:
Name: _____
Phone: _____
Address: _____

IN CASE OF EMERGENCY...

TYPE OF EMERGENCY/DISASTER	PLACE TO MEET OR ACTION TO TAKE

Homeowner/Renter Insurance:
Company: _____
Policy #: _____
Phone: _____

Medical Insurance:
Company: _____
Policy #: _____
Phone: _____

©The Home Hunters Playbook

Daily Tracker Worksheet
Make copies of this and get all your TO DOs done every day!

Date: [_____]   I am Grateful for: [_____]

Top 3 Goals for the day:
1. _____
2. _____
3. _____

Agenda:
__:__ am/pm _____
__:__ am/pm _____
__:__ am/pm _____
__:__ am/pm _____
__:__ am/pm _____
__:__ am/pm _____
__:__ am/pm _____
__:__ am/pm _____
__:__ am/pm _____

To Dos: Priority Level
☐ _____ low med high
☐ _____ low med high
☐ _____ low med high
☐ _____ low med high
☐ _____ low med high
☐ _____ low med high
☐ _____ low med high
☐ _____ low med high
☐ _____ low med high
☐ _____ low med high
☐ _____ low med high
☐ _____ low med high
☐ _____ low med high
☐ _____ low med high

Daily Recap:
Wins: _____
_____

Challenges: _____
_____

Lessons: _____
_____

Intentions: _____
_____

Meal Plan/Diary: H₂O INTAKE
Breakfast _____
Lunch _____
Dinner _____
Snacks _____

30 Minutes of Daily Exercise:
☐ Arms   ☐ Back   ☐ Walk   ☐ Abs
☐ Chest ☐ Legs   ☐ Run   ☐ _____

Household Notes
Keep your notes about your home organized here!

Household Notes
Keep your notes about your home organized here!

SHARE THIS WITH

THE NEXT BUYER

OF YOUR HOME!!!

©The Home Hunters Playbook
©The Home Hunters Playbook

www.ingramcontent.com/pod-product-compliance
Lightning Source LLC
Chambersburg PA
CBHW051926210526
45473CB00006B/2146